SAINTS

SAINTS

Who they are and how they help you

❖

*More than 150 of the heavenly
and holy from St. Agnes to St. Zita*

GENERAL EDITOR
ELIZABETH HALLAM

SIMON & SCHUSTER

New York   London   Toronto   Sydney   Tokyo   Singapore

SIMON & SCHUSTER

Rockefeller Center
1230 Avenue of the Americas
New York, New York 10020

Text copyright © Tessa Clark, Elizabeth Hallam and Cecilia Walters 1994
This edition copyright © Eddison Sadd Editions 1994

All rights reserved including the right of reproduction in whole or in part in any form.

The right of Tessa Clark, Elizabeth Hallam and Cecilia Walters to be
identified as the Authors of this work has been asserted by the Authors
in accordance with the British Copyright, Design and Patents Act 1988.

SIMON & SCHUSTER and colophon are registered trademarks of Simon & Schuster Inc.

Typeset in Berkeley Oldstyle by Create, Bath, UK
Origination by Sele & Color, Rome, Italy
Printed by Dai Nippon Printing Co., Hong Kong

Library of Congress Cataloging in Publication Data

Hallam, Elizabeth M.
    Saints : who they are and how they help you / Elizabeth Hallam.
        p.   cm.
    Includes bibliographical references and index.
    ISBN 0–671–88253–8 : $22.00
    1. Christian patron saints. I. Title.
BX4656.5.H35 1993
282'.092'2–dc20   93–26980
[B]   CIP

FRONTISPIECE: *Altarpiece by Van Eyck from St. Bavo Cathedral, Ghent, showing the Lord
between the Virgin Mary and St. John the Baptist. Below, the Adoration of the Lamb.*

TITLE PAGE: *Detail from the Life of St. Francis of Assisi, a fifteenth-century fresco by Ghirlandaio.*

Contents

✣

INTRODUCTION

✛

WHAT ARE SAINTS?

From the early days of the Christian church saints have played a key role as intercessors between God and mankind, as a source of protection and of miraculous cures. Today new saints are officially recognized by the Church as much because they have lived out the Christian faith at the highest level or have died in its cause, as for their roles as visionaries or wonderworkers—although miracles remain necessary evidence in the process of canonization and new cults, often involving miracles of healing, continue to emerge. Many earlier saints are still venerated and valued for their role as patrons and protectors; others, removed from the official calendars of saints in 1969 because they were deemed fictitious, nevertheless still fascinate and intrigue us.

Some saints—most obviously St. Valentine, St. Christopher and St. Nicholas (Santa Claus)—are deeply embedded in the popular culture of the West, and a great number have long been a potent source of inspiration to artists. Knowledge of their cults and legends therefore allows us a better understanding of some of mankind's greatest artistic achievements.

THE ORIGINS OF SAINTS

The term saint originated in the Latin word *sanctus* (in Greek *hagios*) meaning hallowed or consecrated. The early Christians saw themselves as a community of saints or holy people, but even in the first century they showed special reverence for individuals who, in imitation of Christ, had demonstrated outstanding holiness by dying for their faith.

The Acts of the Apostles sets up a direct parallel between Christ's passion and the death of Stephen—the first Christian martyr and the first to be honored individually as a saint—in c. 35, and for almost four centuries many Christians eagerly sought the martyr's crown. For all this time Christianity remained an outlawed religion in the Roman Empire, which at its greatest extent stretched from Scotland to the River Euphrates in Asia Minor, and from the Straits of Gibraltar to North Africa and the Black Sea.

The memories of the early martyrs were kept vividly alive through their cults. These derived some superficial elements—such as shrines and iconography—from the polytheistic religions of Greece and Rome, but their roots lay in Judaism, with its martyred heroes and prophets, and in the early Christian notions of the rebirth of martyrs even as they died. From the end of the second century, annual celebrations (anniversaries) were held to commemorate the dates of death—known as feast days because death was the beginning of life in heaven—of these witnesses to Christ. Martyrs such as Ignatius of Antioch were invoked to help the living, and their bodily remains or relics were treasured

ABOVE Detail from the Annunciation and the Adoration of the Magi by Fra Angelico.

RIGHT Altarpiece by Giovanni Bellini, in San Giobbe Church, Venice, depicting the Madonna and Child.

and revered. However, the focus on their role as intercessors for the living, the liturgical celebrations at their tombs, the veneration of their relics and a growing stress on miracles disturbed Greco-Roman society and ironically enough encouraged further persecution, creating more martyrs.

When during the reign of Emperor Constantine (312–37) Christianity emerged as the official religion of the Roman Empire, the heroic age of the persecutions was over. Martyrdom continued to be seen as the most glorious way of achieving sainthood, but the accolade of sanctity was extended also to ascetics, who imitated Christ's time of fasting and penitence in the desert, and to confessors and virgins. Thus saints could be monks and nuns, teachers, bishops and people from all walks of life who had not necessarily died for their faith but had borne witness to Christ in the holiness of their lives; and their powers to intercede for the living often matched that of the martyrs.

THE MAKING OF SAINTS

Sainthood was—and still is—established by the process of canonization. In the early churches this was informal, resting largely on popular acclaim, and as a result many early cults of martyrs were founded largely or wholly on the basis of legend. From the fourth century the local bishop would normally approve any new cult, once sanctity had been established by holiness of life or miracles. By the year 1000 papal approval was increasingly being sought out to validate new cults in the Western church, and from the pontificate of Innocent III (1199–1216) all new cults required formal approval by the pope.

Rigorous legal procedures were established to test the validity of the claims of candidates for canonization; these finally crystalized into a fixed process in 1634. At about the same time, beatification—an alternative form of canonization initiated by the bishop and a halfway house to full canonization—was introduced to allow local cults to evolve under the Church's control. The Eastern churches also developed formal procedures for canonization. Protestants, on the other hand, although claiming martyrs for their respective causes and in a few cases showing reverence for some existing cults, have created no new saints of their own. This omission is hardly surprising given their theological opposition to the whole concept of saintly intercession between God and mankind.

PATRON SAINTS, RELICS AND CULTS

Throughout the history of the Western church, the veneration of saints has remained an integral and very popular part of religious devotion. This veneration expresses itself in the form of cults—devotion to saints as the servants of God, second only to the higher devotion accorded to Him. (Throughout this book the term cult is used in this technical and positive sense rather than in its broader modern definition, which often has strong negative connotations.)

Since the days of the early Church, relics—the remains of the saints, and in some cases their clothes and even the instruments of their torture—have assumed an almost talismanic significance. The translations of relics (ceremonial reburials, often in different locations) could be the focus of important ceremonies which in turn might result in new miracles, leading to even greater popularity and veneration. The copious offerings of pilgrims seeking help and intercession meanwhile allowed magnificent basilicas to be built and lavishly ornamented.

A key element in all this devotion is the idea that saints can have a special role as patrons, as guardians and protectors of places and people, and as workers of miraculous cures. Proof of their efficacy was traditionally provided by the saints' Lives, accounts of their deeds and miracles; these hagiographical, stylized and frequently fanciful compositions are usually far more an expression of popular devotion than of historical fact. To some scholars and bishops in the early Church, this reliance on miracles and veneration of relics and tombs smacked of idolatry and of a detraction from the worship of God; but their objections were overcome and saints' cults spread with the Christian faith.

In the later Middle Ages these criticisms resurfaced, and sixteenth-century Renaissance humanists such as Erasmus of Rotterdam, and reformers such as Martin Luther, derided and mocked relics as superstitious practices which were swept away in the fervor of Protestant reform. But in response, the Roman Catholic church of the Counter-Reformation continued to create saints, many in the New World; and in today's world, the papacy continues to recognize many new saints as exemplars of Christian virtue.

SAINTS IN THE MODERN WORLD

Modern canonization processes rely heavily on the use of historical evidence, and seek to distinguish between the verifiable and the legendary aspects of saints' lives and deeds. Very little is known about the real men and women behind some of the more fanciful legends of the early saints. The Bollandists, a society of Jesuit hagiographers which has been working since the 17th century on scholarly editions of the Lives of the saints, pioneered a more critical approach to material which earlier had provided a fertile breeding ground for fantastical fables.

The reform of the Roman calendar in 1969 cut down and standardized feast days; and a core group of saints was selected for universal veneration which represents all periods of history and many different countries of the world. The cults of some saints were restricted to local significance and others—among them Catherine of Alexandria—were quashed altogether on the grounds of lack of evidence. But even as new saints continue to be created, many of the older ones still retain a potent hold on the imagination of people in the late twentieth century.

ABOUT THIS BOOK

Numerous works of reference have been written about the saints, some arranged alphabetically, some by the Church's calendar. The most definitive for the Western church is the 12-volume *Bibliotheca Sanctorum*, written in Italian and published in Rome in 1961. In English, Butler's *Lives of the Saints*, first published in the 1750s, edited and revised by H. Thurston and D. Attwater (4 volumes, 1956), is a magisterial work which includes more than 2,000 saints; D. H. Farmer, *The Oxford Dictionary of Saints* (1992) and D. Attwater,

The Penguin Dictionary of Saints (1983) are briefer and likely to be more generally accessible.

This book draws on material in these and on the best of other such sources, together with detailed monographs and studies of individual saints. Editions of saints' Lives have been consulted as well—among them the Bollandists' great enterprise, the multivolume *Acta Sanctorum*—as has the legendary material which appears in the colorful *Golden Legend* of Jacobus de Voragine (ed. G. Ryan and H. Ripperger, 1941). Where there is disagreement about what constitutes historical evidence, what seems to be the most reliable source is followed.

Despite the careful research which underlies it, this book is not intended primarily as a work of reference. Its focus is on the role of the saints as patrons and protectors and it is arranged by different kinds of patronages and invocations. It looks at the reasons for which saints were—and are—revered for their particular specialities of patronage or protection; or, in the case of some more modern saints, explains which Christian qualities they exemplify. Some saints were regarded as highly efficacious and acquired a variety of patronages; a choice has been made and only one has been explained in each entry, but others have been noted.

A clear distinction is made between historical evidence and legendary material: it is the latter which often explains the patronage. In a few cases entries focus on saints' emblems in art and explain the reasons for their adoption. This underlines the importance and value of visual representations of the saints; and the entries are illustrated from a variety of artistic sources with explanatory captions.

Biographical material is summarized at the end of each entry and is followed as appropriate by information about feast days; cults, relics and pilgrimages; other names; other patronages; and emblems. Further reading is indicated in the bibliography; the most rewarding next step for those who are intrigued and fascinated by these "holy helpers" is to go straight to translations of the original sources and to experience directly their lives and legends.

Elizabeth Hallam
London UK, June 1993

CHAPTER ONE

✛

STATES OF LIFE

To every thing there is a season.
ECCLESIASTES 3:1

✛

LOVE

✛

VALENTINE

(third century)

The patron saint of love has been identified with two early Christians: a priest martyred in Rome in c. 269 and buried on the Flaminian way north of the city, and a bishop of Terni, in Umbria, who was also executed in Rome. Although ecclesiastical authorities in the seventeenth century asserted that they were the same person, some modern experts believe the priest–martyr to be the real Valentine.

The reasons for his association with lovers are also disputed. One possibility is that it derives from the centuries-old belief that birds choose their mates on 14 February, the saint's feast day; another, that it is a survival from the Roman festival of Lupercalia held in mid-February to secure fertility and keep evil away.

What is certain is that troubled lovers have invoked him since medieval times, and that the custom of sending a Valentine's Day card to a chosen partner, first commercialized in the United States in the 1840s, has grown into a major industry.

✛

Third century; identity disputed
FEAST DAY: 14 February

✛

LEFT The Virgin Mary, supreme symbol of motherhood (page 13), suckles the infant Jesus.

Valentine is shown with the birds associated with his feast day; the roses are symbols of love.

FATHERHOOD AND FAMILIES

✛

JOSEPH

(first century)

Husband of the Blessed Virgin Mary and foster father to Jesus, Joseph was, according to the New Testament, betrothed to Mary at the time of the Annunciation. Although descended from David, the

As Jesus' foster father, Joseph had the responsibility of guiding and supporting the holy family—and of educating the young Christ.

✛

king of the Jews, he was poor and a carpenter by trade. St. Matthew's Gospel describes him as a just man and records how his initial distress at Mary's pregnancy was dispelled by an angelic vision; and it tells of how,

after a warning in a dream, he took his family to Egypt to escape Herod's persecution. After the king's death, and again in response to a dream, Joseph returned to Israel. Here, fearing Herod's son, Archelaus, who reigned in Judea, he settled in Nazareth in Galilee.

His last appearance in the New Testament is when he and Mary, on their way back from celebrating the Passover at Jerusalem, are forced to return to the city to find the 12-year-old Jesus who was preaching in the Temple. Most authorities believe that Joseph was dead by the time of the Crucifixion.

In art he is generally depicted as old, but this tradition rests on apocryphal sources; he was more likely to have been a young man at the time of the Nativity. His steadfastness as a guardian and husband is the basis for his patronage of fathers of families.

✛

First century
FEAST DAYS: 19 March; 1 May
CULT: Popular in East from the sixth century, but not widespread in West until the sixteenth; 1 May declared the feast of Joseph the Worker by Pius XII in 1955
OTHER PATRONAGES: Bursars; engineers; house hunters; manual workers, especially carpenters
ALSO INVOKED: By those in doubt; people who desire a holy death

✛

As a child Jesus would have learned carpentry from his foster father. Here Joseph is shown at work—an everyday scene except for the watching angels and the lily, a symbol of chastity, that is in bloom behind Jesus.

MOTHERHOOD
✠
BLESSED VIRGIN MARY
(first century)

As the mother of Jesus, Mary is the most powerful of all the saints; and as the ultimate symbol of motherhood she is invoked to meet every need. But details of her life are sparse.

According to unsubstantiated tradition, she was the daughter of St. Joachim and St. Anne and was presented and dedicated as a virgin at the Temple in Jerusalem. St. Luke's Gospel records that after her betrothal to Joseph, the archangel Gabriel appeared to her at Nazareth to announce that she had been chosen by God to be the mother of Jesus; and that she then visited her cousin Elizabeth, mother of John the Baptist. She and Joseph went to Bethlehem for a tax census after their marriage, and here Jesus was born. The family's flight into Egypt to escape from King Herod is described in St. Matthew's Gospel, as is their return to Nazareth.

Mary remains a shadowy figure in accounts of Christ's public life. She is recorded in the New Testament as visiting Jerusalem at the Passover when Jesus was 12; as attending the marriage at Cana in Galilee when Jesus turned water into wine—his first miracle; as trying to see Jesus while he was teaching; as present at the Crucifixion—"Now there stood by the cross of Jesus his mother,"—when Jesus gave her into the care of St. John the Apostle. It is assumed that from that time she lived in his household.

Mary remained with the apostles after Christ's

This engraving of the Virgin and Child emphasizes the maternal aspect of Mary's relationship with Jesus.

————— ✠ —————

ascension into heaven—the last time she is mentioned in the Bible. Nothing is known of Mary's last years, nor of how or even when she died.

From the fifth century many Christians have believed that she was assumed directly into heaven and that she remained a virgin throughout her life. In 1854 the Roman Catholic church proclaimed that Mary was conceived and born unsoiled by original sin—Immaculate Conception—and (in 1950) that she was taken up into heaven upon her death—Assumption. The "highest of God's creatures," as St. Thomas Aquinas called her, has been the object of special cults and devotions throughout the Christian world and has literally fulfilled her prophecy (Luke 1:48) that "all generations shall call me blessed."

————————— ✠ —————————

First century
PRINCIPAL FEAST DAYS: Purification 2 February;
Annunciation 25 March; Visitation 2 July;
Assumption 15 August; Nativity 8 September;
Immaculate Conception 8 December
CULT: Ubiquitous; some important modern centers
include Loreto (Italy), Lourdes (France), and
Guadalupe (Mexico)
EMBLEM: Normally portrayed holding
her infant son

————————— ✠ —————————

BELOW 'The Adoration of the Magi' is a popular theme in Christian art. In this sixth-century ivory panel the Child raises his hand in a gesture of blessing.

RIGHT Mary, "the highest of God's creatures," has been the object of special cults and devotions throughout the Christian world. This shrine is in Mexico City.

ABOVE A Polish ikon depicting the Virgin and Child. Many Christians have believed that Mary remained a virgin throughout her life.

RIGHT Mary suckles her son in a naturalistic scene by a sixteenth-century Italian artist.

DISCRETION
✛
JOHN OF NEPOMUK
(c. 1345–1393)

The invocation of this saint when discretion is needed is based on a fallacious story—that John was murdered on the orders of Wenceslas IV, king of Bohemia and Holy Roman Emperor, for refusing to divulge the confession of the king's wife, Sophie.

In reality John died because of his involvement in a series of disputes between king and clergy. Educated at the Universities of Prague and Padua and vicar-general to the bishop of Prague from 1389, he was drawn into the bishop's struggles with the king over ecclesiastical rights. Although John was retiring by nature—he repeatedly refused bishoprics that were offered to him—his integrity would not allow him to stand by when he discovered that the king planned to reward an unworthy favorite with an abbey when its aged abbot died. To prevent this, he helped the monks to elect a new abbot so quickly that the news reached Wenceslas at the same time as that of the abbot's death.

On the king's orders John was killed by being burned, then tied to a wheel and thrown off a bridge into the River Moldau. He was buried in St. Vitus' Cathedral in Prague—where he became a symbol of Bohemian nationalism.

According to legend, on the night of John of Nepomuk's death seven stars hovered over the place where he had drowned.

✛

c. 1345 born John Wolflin, Nepomuk, Bohemia; c. 1380 ordained priest; 1387 obtained doctorate of law at the University of Padua; 1389 became vicar-general to John of Genzenstein, bishop of Prague; 20 March 1393 died Prague; 1729 canonized
FEAST DAY: 16 May
CULT: Bohemia/Czechoslovakia
OTHER PATRONAGES: Bohemia; Czechoslovakia; bridges; running water; silence
ALSO INVOKED: Against floods; slander

✛

CHARITABLE GIVING
✛
VINCENT DE PAUL
(1581–1660)

Vincent de Paul's was a life of contrasts. Born into a peasant family in Gascony, France, he was ordained priest in 1601 at the early age of 19 and became a chaplain at the court of Henry IV of France. Here he was falsely accused of theft but remained silent for six months, after which his innocence was proved. His conversion dated from this episode. For the rest of his life, he combined his work among the rich and fashionable with tending society's outcasts: the sick and poverty stricken, galley prisoners and abandoned

Vincent de Paul died more than 300 years ago but the charitable works he inspired have endured.

━━━━━━━━ ✛ ━━━━━━━━

children. Although he was short-tempered and unprepossessing in appearance, Vincent's charisma, his burning love of God, his self-control, sensitivity to the feelings of others and his dedication to relieving human suffering attracted followers from all walks of life: the Church, the fashionable world, slums and prisons.

From 1609 to 1617 Vincent was retained by Philip de Gondi, count of Joigny, as tutor to his children and confessor to his wife. He then worked with the rural poor at Châtillon-les-Dombes and with galley prisoners in Paris. In 1625 he founded, with Madame de Gondi's help, the Vincentian or Lazarist congregation, a society of priests which devoted itself to missionary work especially in small towns and villages. The order's popularity grew rapidly and, in 1633, it was given the priory of Saint-Lazare in Paris, which became its headquarters.

In the same year Vincent founded another congregation, this time together with Louise de Marillac, an aristocratic widow. This was the Sisters of Charity, set up to care for the poor and, especially, to provide hospital care for them.

Vincent's fame grew as a result of these orders and of his many other charitable activities, which included helping victims of the Thirty Years War, in Lorraine, and sending missionaries to Scotland, Ireland and Poland. He was called upon by Louis XIII to help at his deathbed and from 1643 was a valued—if not always heeded—advisor to his widow, Anne of Austria, and her son Louis XIV.

Vincent died in 1660 at the age of nearly 80, and was canonized 77 years later. The charitable lay society of Saint-Vincent-de-Paul was founded in 1833 by Frederick Ozanam in Paris, and in 1885 Pope Leo XIII named St. Vincent patron of all charitable societies.

━━━━━━━━ ✛ ━━━━━━━━

1581 born Ranquine, Gascony (now Saint-Vincent-de-Paul, Landes); 1593 began education with Franciscans at Dax; from 1597 attended Toulouse University; 1601 ordained priest; 1609 confessor and tutor to the Gondi family; 1617 parish priest of Châtillon-les-Dombes; 1622 missions to convicts in Bordeaux; 1625 founded Vincentian (Lazarist) congregation; 1633 founded Sisters of Charity; 1660 died Paris; 1737 canonized
FEAST DAY: 27 September (formerly 19 July)

━━━━━━━━ ✛ ━━━━━━━━

PROMPT SOLUTIONS
✛
EXPEDITUS
(existence unlikely)

It is unlikely that Expeditus existed. Some martyrologies and calendars claim that his name is a play on the word expedite (expeditiously)—an example of the patronage coming before the saint. Others suggest that his name is a misreading of Elpidius, another martyr in the group with which he was venerated. Nevertheless, his cult was widespread from the Middle Ages, particularly in Sicily and southern Germany.

━━━━━━━━ ✛ ━━━━━━━━

Existence unlikely
FEAST DAY: 19 April
CULT: Widespread from Middle Ages
OTHER PATRONAGES: Merchants; navigators

━━━━━━━━ ✛ ━━━━━━━━

LOST CAUSES
✠
JUDE
(first century)

One of the twelve apostles, Jude, also called Thaddeus, is generally thought to have been the brother of another apostle, St. James the Less, and the author of the epistle of Jude in the New Testament. Tradition has it that he preached the gospel with St. Simon in Syria and Mesopotamia. He finally went to Persia where he was martyred with arrows or javelins, or on a cross.

He was venerated in the Middle Ages, but his cult later suffered as his name became confused with that of Judas Iscariot, Christ's betrayer. Because of this resemblance, for many centuries no one would invoke him for anything—hence his willingness to help people even in the most desperate situations.

✠

First century
FEAST DAY: 28 October
CULT: Venerated in Middle Ages in Reims and Toulouse in France, and at Saint Peter's, Rome, where Jude's and Simon's relics were reputedly translated in the seventh or eighth century

✠

This alabaster statuette of Jude shows the saint carrying an oar and an anchor. Although the latter is a Christian symbol of hope—fittingly enough for the patron of lost causes—the anchor and oar may allude to the belief that Jude's early life was spent as a fisherman.

RIGHT *Peter holds the golden key to heaven. Over the centuries artists have consistently depicted him as elderly and balding, with a short, curly beard.*

LONGEVITY
✠
PETER
(died c. 64)

St. Peter was Jesus' most prominent disciple and became the leader of the apostles after Christ's death. He first appears in the New Testament as a fisherman named Simon, making his living from the Sea of Galilee. His brother, Andrew, introduced him to Jesus, who declared that he would make both brothers fishers of men. Later in his ministry Jesus renamed Simon as Cephas (Peter), meaning rock, as he would be the rock upon which the Church would be built. Like the other apostles he would have the power of binding and loosing, but he alone would be given the keys to the gates of heaven.

In the New Testament, Peter is always listed first among the disciples and witnessed the most important events of Jesus' ministry. Although he betrayed Jesus by denying all knowledge of him to the officials of the

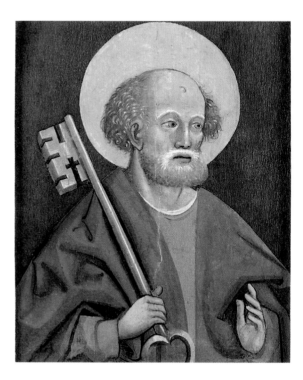

*The portrayal of Peter's
martyrdom by Michelangelo.*

✦

Jewish high priest, after the Resurrection Jesus appeared to him before any other apostle, and again enjoined him to care for the Church ("Feed my sheep. Feed my lambs.") Peter obeyed these instructions, preaching to crowds, performing miracles in Christ's name, surviving imprisonment by Herod Agrippa and making missionary visits to Samaria and Antioch, where he was the city's first bishop.

The New Testament does not throw any light on the ancient tradition that Peter ministered also in Rome, where in Emperor Nero's reign he was martyred by being crucified head down. However, several near-

LEFT Saint Peter's, Rome; the first church on its site was reputedly built over the saint's grave.

This sixteenth-century statuette shows Peter wearing a cloak and tunic. Other artists have portrayed him in ecclesiastical clothes; although there is no firm proof, early writers record his presence in Rome and imply that he founded the Church there.

contemporary sources record his presence there and state that he founded the Church of Rome, was martyred and was buried in the Vatican area. No other church apart from Saint Peter's, Rome, claims his relics, and his place as Rome's first bishop remains uncorroborated but probable.

Among the multitude of writings attributed to St. Peter, only two—the Gospel of Mark and the First Epistle of Peter—are likely to have been composed or influenced directly by him.

He is venerated as the doorkeeper of heaven—the reason he is invoked for a long life—and as the patron of the Church and the papacy.

FEAST DAY: 29 June
CULT: Widespread throughout the Church since the third century
OTHER PATRONAGES: The Church; the papacy
EMBLEMS: Keys; a book

CURES FROM PAIN
✢
MADRON
(?sixth century)

The town of Madron, in Cornwall, England, takes its name from a mythical sixth-century monk who settled and died there. According to one tradition this Madron can be identified as Medran (died c. 540), a disciple of the Irish bishop St. Ciaran of Saighar, whom he accompanied on a mission to Cornwall. Less likely tales equate Madron with the Cornish St. Piran or the Welsh St. Paternus. What is certain is that St. Madron's altar, chapel and well have been associated with miraculous cures from pain and illness over many centuries. In art he is represented as an abbot holding a lighted lamp.

?Sixth century
FEAST DAY: 17 May
CULT: In St. Madron, Cornwall
EMBLEM: Lighted lamp

SAFE TRAVEL
✛
CHRISTOPHER
(?third century)

The only known fact about Christopher is that he was martyred in Asia Minor; a church in Bithynia, now northern Turkey, was dedicated to him in c. 450. The rest is legend, the best-known strand of which describes him as a man gigantic in stature and frightening in form, whose name was Offero. In his youth he offered his services to the devil, who appeared to him as a knight on a black charger, but decided to seek Christ when this demonic master fled at the sight of a white cross.

A hermit who instructed him in Christianity assigned him the task of living near a river and carrying people across—the reason why he is invoked on behalf of travelers.

One stormy night his burden was a child who became steadily heavier until Offero was bowed down with his weight. When they reached the opposite bank, the child revealed himself as Jesus Christ and told Offero that from now on his name would be Christopher (*Christophoros* in Greek means Christ bearer). Jesus also instructed him to recross the river and replant his staff in the ground, where it would bear flowers and dates the next day.

Christopher is then said to have preached the gospel in Lycia, in Asia Minor. Here he was arrested for refusing to sacrifice to the Roman gods and, while in prison, converted two women who were sent to seduce him.

He was condemned to be put to death, first by fire

Christopher carries Christ on his shoulders; the staff he will plant on the river bank is already bearing leaves and fruit.

————— ✛ —————

and then by arrows, but miraculously neither harmed him. Finally he was beheaded.

Very popular in the Middle Ages, Christopher was invoked against water, plague and tempests as well as by travelers. His cult declined in the seventeenth century, but revived again dramatically in the twentieth to protect travelers by road and air.

In Paris, a church close to the Citroën car factory on the quai de Javel was dedicated to St. Christopher. This patronage, which has survived the reduction of his cult to local status in 1969, is based on the belief that anyone who sees an image of the saint will not die on that day.

For that reason, the countless paintings, statues and other visual representations of St. Christopher to be found in churches are often placed close to the main door or on the north wall facing the entrance, or located in such a way as to be in full view of worshippers.

————————— ✛ —————————

?Third century
FEAST DAY: 25 July
CULT: Very popular in Middle Ages;
declined from seventeenth century
and revived in the twentieth.
Reduced to local status in 1969
ALSO INVOKED: Against water; plague; tempest

————————— ✛ —————————

·ST. CHRISTOPHER·

ABOVE *The devil cowers in terror at the sight of a white cross. Early legends record that Christopher, searching for the most powerful king in the world, offered his services to Satan, but decided to seek Christ instead when he saw his master's fear of Christianity's symbol.*

LEFT *Through the centuries most representations of Christopher have shown him carrying Christ on his shoulders. This modern medallion, from Italy, follows tradition in depicting the saint as bearded and carrying a staff.*

BELOW *This illustration emphasizes Christopher's great height (he was said to be more than 20 feet tall) and contrasts his stature with the size of the child he bears on his back—whose weight nevertheless bows him down as he crosses the river.*

ABOVE *Christopher was a popular subject for wall paintings in medieval churches, particularly in England. The size of his images—which are often very large in order to be immediately visible to anyone entering the building—may account for the stories of his immense height. This thirteenth-century wall painting is in a church in Buckinghamshire.*

SAFE MOTORING
✛
FRANCES OF ROME
(1384–1440)

Frances was born into a noble Roman family and was brought up in a luxurious but pious household in the Trastevere district of Rome. In 1396, when she was barely 13, her parents married her to Lorenzo Ponziano, whose family was as wealthy and as aristocratic as hers.

Although Frances had known since the age of 11 that her real desire was to be a nun, she was a model wife, bearing her husband several children and, from the age of 17, running a household that included her brother-in-law Paluzzo and his wife Vanozza. Throughout their life, Lorenzo repaid Frances's devotion with a love and reverence that only increased during the 40 years they were married.

Soon after her marriage Frances discovered that Vanozza shared her ideals, and the two women visited and cared for the poor and sick of Rome. They continued their ministry even after 1408 when the city was invaded by Ladislas of Naples, an ally of the antipope, who plundered the Ponziano palace in 1409, driving Lorenzo into exile and destroying the family's possessions in the surrounding countryside. Frances's prayers and labors were rewarded with the gift of healing and, in c. 1414 (the year Lorenzo returned from exile), a constant vision of her guardian angel. His light enabled her to see at night—the basis for her patronage of motorists, assigned in 1925.

In 1425, Frances founded a secular society of devout women, the Oblates of the Tor de' Specchi—the name came from the house in which they lived—to care for the poor; and 11 years later, after Lorenzo's death, she herself entered this community which still flourishes to this day.

She died in 1440, a strange light on her face and with the words: "The angel has finished his task; he beckons me to follow him." She was canonized by Pope Paul V in 1608. Her relics rest in the church where she was buried, in Rome, and which now bears her name.

✛

1384 born Rome; 1396 married Lorenzo Ponziano; 1400 birth of first child, John Baptist; 1401 became head of Ponziano household; 1425 founded Oblates of the Tor de' Specchi; 1436 entered community; 1440 died; 1608 canonized
FEAST DAY: 9 March
OTHER PATRONAGE: Widows

✛

SAFE SEAFARING
✛
FRANCIS OF PAOLA
(1416–1507)

The son of humble and pious parents in Calabria, Italy, Francis was named after St. Francis of Assisi. He was only 14 when he was inspired to become a hermit by a pilgrimage with his parents to Assisi, Monte Cassino and Rome. At first he lived alone in a cave overlooking the sea, near his home town of Paola; then he was joined by two companions for whom the local people built a chapel and cells. Attracted by the asceticism and simplicity of the life, others joined the group and, in 1436, the archbishop of Cozenza gave it his approval. Many miracles were recorded as other communities sprang up in southern Italy, and in 1474 Pope Sixtus IV approved the new order as the Franciscan Minim Friars.

Francis's fame spread outside Italy when, in 1483, Louis XI of France realized he was mortally ill and summoned Francis to heal him. Francis went reluctantly and only on Pope Sixtus IV's instructions, and by his prayers and example persuaded the king to resign himself to dying.

After Louis' death, in the same year, the king's successors, the regent Anne of Beaujeu and his son Charles VIII, asked Francis to stay in France. He remained there for the rest of his life.

As well as conducting diplomatic negotiations with Brittany and Spain and acting for a while as tutor to Charles VIII, Francis perfected his rule and widened it to include women and the laity. He died in 1507 and was buried at Plessis-les-Tours; his canonization

Francis of Paola attracted followers by the extreme austerity of his Rule and was famous for his prophecies and ability to read minds.

---

followed five years later, in 1512. Because so many of his miracles were connected with the sea—one describes how he sailed across the Straits of Messina on his cloak—he was declared the patron saint of seafarers by Pope Pius XII in 1943.

1416 born Paola, Calabria; 1429 became a hermit; 1436 archbishop of Cozenza approved his congregation; 1474 Pope Sixtus IV approved the Order of Minims; 1483 on Sixtus IV's orders traveled to France; 1507 died near Tours, France; 1512 canonized by Pope Julius II; 1943 declared patron saint of seafarers
FEAST DAY: 2 April
CULT: Widespread in Italy, France, Mexico
ALSO INVOKED: Against plague; sterility

RACIAL HARMONY
✛
MARTIN DE PORRES
(1579–1639)

Martin was born in Lima, Peru, one of two natural children of John de Porres, a Spanish knight, and Anna Velasquez, his mistress, a Panamanian of African descent. Although de Porres acknowledged Martin as his child, he was embarrassed by the boy's dark complexion and left him to Anna's care. She apprenticed him to a barber surgeon in c. 1582; but three years later, at the age of 15, he joined the Dominicans. As a lay brother, he worked as a gardener, barber and farm laborer.

Martin served the people of the city as well as the members of the order, in a ministry that was as practical as it was selflessly dedicated. He established an orphanage in Lima, and used the skills he had learned during his apprenticeship to nurse the city's sick, caring for the plague-stricken and the poor whatever their race or their color.

He was particularly concerned for the welfare of the black slaves who had been brought to Peru from Africa. Nor was his immediate family ignored: he raised a dowry for his niece and helped to solve difficulties in his sister's marriage.

All animals were also the beneficiaries of his charity: he forgave rats and mice for the damage they did, explaining that there was not enough for them to eat, and kept a "home" for abandoned cats and dogs in his sister's house.

A modest man, he described himself as a "mulatto dog." But he won the respect and admiration of people from all walks of life, and his community—which knew him as "father of charity"—accepted him as its director. He was credited with supernatural powers during his life, and miraculous cures were reported at his tomb.

Nevertheless, more than three centuries elapsed before Martin's canonization in 1962. At the same time, he was recognized as the patron saint of racial harmony for his service to all men and women regardless of race.

1579 born Lima, Peru; c.1583 apprenticed to
barber-surgeon; 1586 entered Rosary convent
of the Friars Preachers, Lima;
1639 died; 1962 canonized
FEAST DAY: 5 November
OTHER PATRONAGES: Social justice; public
education, television, public health (Peru); people
of mixed race

*Martin de Porres' mother was a freed woman, and
throughout his life he worked for the welfare of
Peru's many African slaves, whose owners had the
power of life—and even death—over them.*

NATIVE RIGHTS
+
TURIBIUS
(1538–1606)

Turibius, archbishop of Lima, is one of Latin
America's best-known saints and stands as an
exemplar of the championship of native rights. Born of
a noble family at Mayorga in Spain, he was religious as
a child and youth but never considered becoming a
priest. Instead he studied law at the Universities of
Valladolid and Salamanca. His brilliance as a lawyer
attracted the attention of Philip II, king of Spain, who
in 1573 appointed him principal judge of the court of
the Inquisition at Granada—unusually, since Turibius
was a layman. Five years later, when he was 40, the
king appointed him archbishop of Lima in the Spanish
colony of Peru. Although Turibius was shocked by,
and appealed against, the decision, he was overruled.
He eventually took holy orders and was consecrated as
archbishop, arriving in Lima in 1581.

His task was daunting. The archbishopric of Peru
was vast—400 miles of coast stretching inland to the
Andes—and was dominated by extortionate and tyrannical Spanish governors, often supported by lazy
and rapacious clerics. Turibius visited the whole of his
diocese over the next seven years and tried to correct
the worst clerical abuses. He called a provincial council
in 1583 which laid down the lines of future development for the Church in South America, and in 1591
founded a seminary in Lima to train priests—the first
in the New World.

There was great opposition to Turibius from the
governors of Peru whose authority he challenged. He
learned local dialects so that he could communicate
with—and convert—the native peoples; and he was a
strong and effective champion of their rights. He died
in 1606 at Santa and was canonized in 1726.

+

*RIGHT Workers in modern Peru; Turibius' first journey
through his huge diocese took seven years and he
found that many of the Indians who had been baptized
knew almost nothing about Christianity.*

1538 born Mayorga, near León, Spain; 1562 completed studies at University of Valladolid; 1568 completed study of law at University of Salamanca; 1573 principal judge in the court of the Inquisition at Granada; 1578–9 took holy orders; 1579 consecrated archbishop of Lima; 1581 arrived in Peru; 1581–8 visitation of diocese; 1591 founded seminary at Lima; 1606 died Santa, Peru; 1679 beatified; 1726 canonized
FEAST DAY: 23 March
CULT: Mainly in South America; now more widespread because of his pioneering reforms, and to represent South America

✛

NATIVE TRADITIONS
✛
MARTYRS OF PARAGUAY
(died 1628)

Rocco Gonzalez, Alonso Rodriguez and Juan de Castillo were Jesuit missionaries opposed to colonialism, whose work among the native tribes of Paraguay and Brazil led to their martyrdom.

Gonzalez, their leader, a Spaniard of noble descent who had been born in Paraguay, ministered to the Indian tribes from 1609. After 1611 he was prominent in setting up the Paraguayan Reductions—settlements of native peoples run by the missionaries who acted as trustees of them and their native traditions. The Reductions stood firm against the imperialism of the Spanish conquerors and the activities of the Inquisition and, as a result, were suppressed in the eighteenth century.

Gonzalez and his two companions were killed by hostile Indians in 1628, while setting up a new Reduction in a remote area near Caaro (now in Brazil). A local witch doctor roused opposition to them and on 15 November, Gonzalez was murdered with tomahawks while hanging a church bell. Rodriguez died when he came to help and both bodies were burned. De Castillo, returning two days later, was stoned to death. Evidence about the killings was lost for some two centuries, but following its rediscovery, the three martyrs were beatified in 1934 and canonized in 1988.

✛

November 1628 died Caaro, Brazil
FEAST DAY: 17 November

✛

LEFT *The three martyrs used rivers like this tributary of the Amazon to reach the tribal peoples of Brazil and Paraguay.*

RIGHT *This carving of Christ wearing the crown of thorns was made by the guarani Indians of Paraguay in the seventeenth century— possibly at a time when the martyrs were establishing the Reductions.*

CHAPTER TWO

✢

WOMEN

Her price is far above rubies.
PROVERBS 31:10

———————— ✢ ————————

YOUNG GIRLS

✢

AGNES

(died c. 305)

One of the most celebrated of early Roman martyrs, Agnes is also one of the least well documented. All that is known of her for certain is that she was killed for her faith, that she was buried beside Rome's Via Nomentana and that a church was built over her grave in c. 354. According to a later, fifth-century account of her martyrdom, she was 13 years old when she refused to marry, declaring that she was dedicated to Christ and preferred death to losing her virginity. She offered herself as a martyr and was executed in the Roman manner by being stabbed in the throat. Her youthfulness and steadfast courage have made her one of the most popular saints. Because of her chastity, she is the patron of young girls.

———————— ✢ ————————

c. 305 died
FEAST DAY: 21 January
CULT: Ancient and widespread
OTHER PATRONAGES: Betrothed couples;
gardeners; bodily purity
ALSO INVOKED: For chastity
EMBLEM: Lamb

———————— ✢ ————————

LEFT Anne was the Virgin Mary's mother and is invoked during pregnancy (page 32).

This painting of Agnes, a virgin martyr, shows her emblem, a white lamb, at her feet.

WIVES
✛
MONICA
(332–387)

Mother of the eminent theologian St. Augustine, Monica is the special patron of married women and a pattern for motherhood. She lived at Tagaste in North Africa (today Souk Ahras in Algeria), and was married to Patricius, a violent-tempered and dissolute man. Her problems were made worse by the presence of her hostile mother-in-law in her house, and she took to alcohol as a refuge.

Eventually she overcame this addiction, and by her patience and loving kindness converted Patricius to Christianity in 370. He died a holy death the next year,

and she then tried to convert Augustine—who at that time was leading a life of debauchery and self-indulgence. To escape his mother's ministrations he fled to Italy in 383, but Monica followed him, first to Rome and then to Milan. Here, with the help of St. Ambrose, Augustine accepted the Christian faith in 386 and was baptized in the following year. Monica is said to have declared that all her hopes had now been fulfilled and that she had no more need for a life on earth; and soon afterwards, as she and her son were making their return journey to Africa, she died at Ostia in Italy.

✛

332 born ?Tagaste, Algeria; 370 husband Patricius received baptism and 371 died; 383 followed Augustine to Italy; 387 Augustine baptized; Monica died Ostia
FEAST DAY: 27 August
CULT: Monica's relics were translated to Arrouaise, France, and her cult was popularized by the Arrouaisian canons; more relics were translated from Ostia to Rome in 1430 and her cult grew there
OTHER PATRONAGE: Mothers
EMBLEMS: Girdle; tears

✛

Monica with a youthful St. Augustine; the strength of her belief converted her husband and influenced her son's decision to become a Christian.

PREGNANCY
✛
ANNE
(first century)

There are no historical details of the life of the mother of the Blessed Virgin Mary—even her name, Anne, like that of Mary's father, Joachim, comes from an apocryphal source, the second-century Gospel of James.

According to tradition, Anne and her husband had no children, even after many years of marriage. Shamed by their childlessness, Joachim fasted and prayed in the desert for 40 days, while Anne prayed beneath a laurel bush. Both saw angelic visions in which they were assured that they would have a child, and in due course Mary was born to them. As the mother of Mary, Anne has a particular responsibility for pregnant women.

An angel appears to Anne, mother of the Virgin Mary. Although nothing is known for certain about Mary's parents, Anne has been worshipped since the sixth century. In the West her cult became especially popular during the fourteenth century. It was later attacked by Martin Luther.

First century
FEAST DAY: 26 July
CULT: Sixth century in Eastern church; from eighth century in Western church; widespread since fourteenth century; extended by the papacy to the whole Western church in 1584

CHILDBIRTH

RAYMOND NONNATUS
(1204–1240)

Raymond was born by Caesarean section after his mother's death in labor—hence his surname (*non natus* means "not born") and his patronage of childbirth. According to tradition he was a native of Catalonia, Spain, who became a member of the Mercedarian Order founded to ransom Christian captives of the Moors of North Africa. Ordained priest in 1222, he became master-general of the order and went to North Africa to carry out its work. There he was so distressed by the plight of the prisoners that, when his money ran out, he surrendered himself as a hostage to secure the freedom of just one more slave.

Raymond suffered in captivity under the Moors for many years—his mouth is said to have been padlocked to prevent him from preaching to his fellow captives. Eventually he was ransomed by his order and in 1239 went home to Spain where he was nominated cardinal by Pope Gregory IX. He died near Barcelona on his way to Rome. Many miracles were attributed to him both in life and after his death.

1204 born Portello, Catalonia; 1222 ordained priest; 1239 nominated cardinal; 1240 died Cardona near Barcelona
FEAST DAY: 31 August
CULT: 1969 reduced to local status
OTHER PATRONAGES: Midwives; children; pregnant women

BREAST FEEDING
+
GILES
(died c. 710)

One of the most popular medieval saints, Giles was born probably in Provence, and founded an important monastery at Saint-Gilles, on the banks of the Rhône.

According to later legend, Giles was an Athenian who traveled to southern France where he became a hermit, taking his nourishment from the milk of a hind—the basis for his patronage of breast feeding and nursing mothers. One day the hind was hunted by Wamba, the local Visigothic king, and took refuge with Giles. The king shot at her with an arrow which wounded and crippled her protector—hence Giles is also the patron of the physically disabled.

A window in St. Giles, Cripplegate, London—one of many churches dedicated to the saint.

+

Giles with the hind that nourished him with its milk during his years as a hermit.

Giles is said to have traveled to Rome to offer his monastery to the pope, who granted him privileges and protection and gave him two doors made from cypress wood. Giles threw these into the River Tiber, and found them waiting for him on his return to Saint-Gilles, on a beach near his monastery.

c. 710 died
FEAST DAY: 1 September
CULT: Widely popular in Middle Ages; local status since 1969
OTHER PATRONAGES: The physically disabled; beggars; blacksmiths; woods; Edinburgh
ALSO INVOKED: Against epilepsy; cancer; insanity; sterility in women; terrors of the night
EMBLEMS: Hind; arrow

HOUSEWIVES

MARTHA

(first century)

Martha was the sister of Lazarus, whom Jesus raised from the dead, and of Mary of Bethany (who is widely identified with Mary Magdalene). The New Testament describes her solicitude when Jesus visited the family home—the basis for her patronage of housewives—and also records her faith in him as the Christ and the Son of God which she affirmed before he restored Lazarus to life. There is a final mention of Martha, again in a housewifely role, serving supper to Jesus a few days before the Crucifixion. Nothing else is known of her life, or her death. A medieval legend connects her, Lazarus and Mary Magdalene with an early mission to Provence.

First century
FEAST DAY: 29 July
CULT: Widespread; Martha's supposed relics, discovered at Tarascon, Provence, in 1187, became the basis of a local cult
OTHER PATRONAGES: Innkeepers; cooks; servants; lay sisters
EMBLEMS: Keys; a broom; a ladle; a dragon (from Provençal legend)

Martha and her sister Mary kneel at Jesus' feet in a medieval portrayal of the raising of Lazarus. A Provençal legend describes how the two sisters later accompanied Lazarus on a mission to France, where Martha overcame a dragon by sprinkling holy water over it.

COOKS
+
LAURENCE
(died 258)

The most celebrated of all Roman martyrs, Laurence was one of the seven deacons of Rome and was put to death a few days after Pope Sixtus II, during the Valerian persecution. He was buried beside the road to Tivoli and the basilica of St. Laurence Outside the Walls was constructed over his tomb.

Although most modern authorities agree that Laurence was beheaded, the legend that he was roasted alive on a grid attained such credence that from the fourth century his emblem has been a gridiron. The

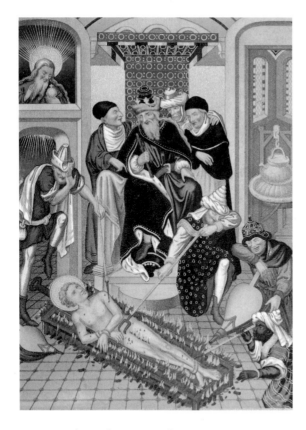

Artists have often portrayed Laurence as a young man, who remains calm during his ordeal.

link between this and his patronage of cooks is clear.

The reason given for Laurence's martyrdom is equally legendary, but more credible. According to tradition, when the prefect of Rome demanded that he hand over the Church's treasure, Laurence gathered together the city's poor and suffering and presented them to the official with the words: "Here is the Church's treasure."

+

258 died
FEAST DAY: 10 August
CULT: Strong throughout Christian world from the
fourth century
OTHER PATRONAGES: Brewers; confectioners;
cutlers; armorers; schoolboys; students;
washerwomen; glaziers
EMBLEMS: Gridiron; purse of money

+

WIDOWS
+
PAULA
(347–404)

The patron saint of widows was herself widowed at the age of 32 when her husband, a Roman senator, died leaving her with five children. During the long period of grief that followed she was helped and influenced by two other future saints: the learned biblical scholar Jerome, who later wrote her biography, and Marcella, also a widow. Paula was one of a group of Roman women, all dedicated Christians, who met at Marcella's house to be instructed by Jerome. Others included two of her children: Eustochium and Blaesilla, a young widow who died when she was 20. Both were later recognized as saints.

When Jerome left Rome in 385 to settle near Bethlehem, Paula followed him with Eustochium and, after a pilgrimage in the Holy Land, in 386 became the

+

Paula was St. Jerome's pupil and followed him to the Holy Land. Fluent in Greek, she also learned Hebrew to improve her understanding of the scriptures.

leader of the women in his group. She was the moving force in building a convent for them, as well as a monastery for the men and a hospice for pilgrims. She was also in charge of Jerome's welfare.

Paula was said to have been efficient, tactful, scholarly—she was fluent in Greek and Hebrew—and practical. She was also extravagant in her gifts to charity (Eustochium was left with a large debt when Paula died) and alarmed Jerome with the extent of her self-mortification. Her remarkable career after the death of her husband singled her out as the patron saint of widows.

She died at the age of 56 and was buried beneath the Church of the Nativity at Nazareth.

---

347 born Rome; 379 widowed; 385 left Rome; 386 went to Bethlehem; 404 died Bethlehem
FEAST DAY: 26 January
CULT: Ancient and became widespread

UNHAPPY MARRIAGES
✛
WILGEFORTIS
(legendary)

The legend of Wilgefortis—which is entirely without foundation—describes her as a septuplet daughter of a king of Portugal. Although her father was pagan she and her brothers and sisters became Christians, and she vowed that she would remain a virgin all her life. Knowing that she had sworn this oath, her father nevertheless promised her in marriage to the king of Sicily. Wilgefortis prayed for help in her predicament and, as a result, grew a beard and moustache.

The Sicilian king was so repelled by her appearance that he withdrew his suit and, in revenge, her father had her crucified.

The legendary Wilgefortis' dying prayers on the cross, that all who remembered her should be freed of their troubles and encumbrances, are the reason that she has been invoked by men and women trapped in unhappy marriages.

Her patronage in England, where she is known as St. Uncumber, is more specific: she is called upon by women who want to rid themselves of their troublesome husbands.

Legendary
FEAST DAY: 20 July
ALSO KNOWN AS: Uncumber
CULT: Originated probably in fourteenth-century Flanders; found widely in western Europe in later Middle Ages. Suppressed in 1969.

RECONCILING UNHAPPILY MARRIED
✛
THEODORE OF SYKEON
(died 613)

Theodore's mother was a publican and brothel keeper at Sykeon in Galatia (modern Turkey), his father an acrobat in a circus; but Theodore's life was changed when he was six years old and Stephen, a talented cook, arrived at the inn. The superb food he produced attracted so many customers that Theodore's mother, grandmother and aunt were able to stop working as prostitutes; and the newcomer's devout Christianity soon converted the young boy.

Theodore was ordained priest at the early age of 18 and became a monk on a pilgrimage to Jerusalem. On his return he installed himself as a hermit near Sykeon, where he endured spectacular, self-imposed penances, such as being fettered and shut in a cage suspended above his cave in a cliff face for many weeks at a time. Such was his fame as a healer and miracle worker that many followers congregated, for whom he built a monastery.

He was elected as bishop of Anastasiopolis in Galatia in about 590, but resigned in about 600 and again became a hermit, this time at Acrena near Heliopolis (now Baalbek, Lebanon). There he stayed, apart from a brief visit to Constantinople, until his death in c. 613. His miracles were numerous, and included curing the emperor's son of elephantiasis, warding off plagues of locusts, beetles and mice, and reconciling unhappily married couples—the reason for his patronage. He is also known to have fostered the cult of St. George.

———————— ✛ ————————

Ordained priest aged 18;
hermit at Mossyna, near Sykeon;
c. 590 became bishop of Anastasiopolis;
c. 600 resigned and became a hermit
at Acrena; c. 613 died;
relics moved to Constantinople
FEAST DAY: 22 April

———————— ✛ ————————

WOMEN
WANTING SONS
✛
FELICITY
(died ?165)

Accoding to tradition, Felicity was a rich Roman widow who had given birth to seven boys—the reason she is invoked by women wanting sons. When they grew to adulthood they became, like her, devout Christians; and when the family was arrested for its

———————— ✛ ————————

*The legend of Felicity describes
how she and her seven sons
were condemned to death because
they refused to deny their
Christian faith and sacrifice to
the Roman gods. The brothers were
the first to die: Felicity was
forced to watch their executions
before she herself was martyred.*

———————— ✛ ————————

beliefs, they followed her example and refused to sacrifice to the pagan gods. As a result they and their mother were martyred.

Behind this story very little is known of the historical Felicity, except that she was martyred on 23 November in an unknown year and buried on the Via Salaria in Rome. Although there is also evidence that seven martyrs were buried in the city on 10 July, year again unknown, there is none that they were brothers or that they had any connection with Felicity.

✛

?165 died Rome; buried Via Salaria
FEAST DAY: 23 November
CULT: Early and widespread. Confined to local calendar since 1969
EMBLEMS: Sword; seven sons

✛

DESPAIRING PROSTITUTES
✛
MARGARET OF CORTONA
(1247–1297)

Margaret was the beautiful and high-spirited daughter of a peasant farmer in Tuscany. Her mother died when she was seven years old and at the age of 18, after many years of ill-treatment by her father's new wife, she was ripe for seduction. She met a young nobleman from Montepulciano, bore him a son and lived openly with him until his murder nine years later. Denied refuge by her father and stepmother, she turned to the Franciscan friars for help and was given a home with a family in Cortona. The general transformation that followed, from self-indulgent kept woman to self-mortifying penitent, is the basis of her patronage of prostitutes who despair of changing their way of life.

Margaret performed penances in public, as when she appeared at mass at Laviano, her birthplace, with a halter round her neck, begging for forgiveness. The Franciscans had also to restrain her from mutilating her face, but despite her excesses she was eventually admitted to the Third Order of St. Francis. Until her

Margaret of Cortona compensated for her early sinfulness by committing herself to a life of penance and self-mortification.

✛

death in 1297 she led a life of extreme austerity—she allowed herself little food or sleep and wore a hair shirt—and devoted herself to caring for the poor and sick, for whom she founded a hospice in 1286.

Some local people doubted that she had truly repented and there were rumors of a relationship between her and one of the friars. Nevertheless her prayers and advice converted many sinners and many miraculous cures are attributed to her.

✛

1247 born Laviano, Tuscany; 1265–74 lived with nobleman until his death; 1297 died Cortona; 1728 canonized
FEAST DAY: 22 February

✛

REPENTANT PROSTITUTES
✦
MARY MAGDALENE
(first century)

In the New Testament Mary Magdalene appears as one of Jesus' most devoted followers, whose "seven devils" were cast out by him. She watched by the cross at the Crucifixion, attended his burial and later, when she went to anoint his body, found the tomb empty. The risen Christ then appeared to her.

The widespread tradition that identifies her with the unnamed repentant prostitute who anointed Jesus' feet with ointment from an alabaster box has been repudiated by the Church. Its widespread currency in the Middle Ages, however, made Mary Magdalene patron saint of penitent sinners and of repentant prostitutes.

A pensive Mary Magdalene; one of her patronages is the contemplative life.

✦

✦

First century
FEAST DAY: 22 July
CULT: Widespread
in East and West;
popular in Provence which,
according to legend, was
evangelized by Mary Magdalene,
her brother Lazarus
and her sister Martha;
relics claimed by Abbey of
Vézelay in France
from the eleventh century
OTHER PATRONAGES:
The contemplative life; penitent
sinners
EMBLEM: Alabaster box
of ointment

✦

✦

According to legend Mary Magdalene spent the last 30 years of her life as a hermit on a French mountain. The book she is reading in this engraving rests on a skull—a symbol of death.

✦

MARIA ERGO ACCEPIT LIBRAM VNGUETI NARDI PISTICI PCIOSE ET VXIT PEDES IHV

LEFT *Mary Magdalene before her conversion; the alabaster jar contains the ointment with which she anointed Jesus' feet.*

BELOW Mary Magdalene kneels by Christ's empty tomb. The simple cloak she is wearing denotes her status as a penitent.

RIGHT In this crucifixion from a sixteenth-century altarpiece Mary Magdalene is portrayed in traditional style, wearing a red dress and with long, flowing hair.

BELOW In this fourth-century ivory panel Mary Magdalene is depicted kneeling at Jesus' feet. Her sister, Martha, is on the left.

CHAPTER THREE

✛

CHILDREN

... the days of your youth, while the evil days come not.
ECCLESIASTES 12:1

———— ✛ ————

BIRTH
✛
MARGARET OF ANTIOCH
(existence unlikely)

Although Pope Gelasius I declared her story apocryphal in 494, Margaret went on to become one of the most popular saints of the Middle Ages. She was said to have been the Christian daughter of a pagan priest, Aesidius of Antioch, during the reign of the Roman emperor Diocletian. When she rejected the suit of the prefect Olybrius, he denounced her as a Christian, and she was subjected to a series of extraordinary ordeals, including being swallowed by Satan in the shape of a dragon. Eventually she and her many followers were beheaded.

Margaret is said to have promised, just before she died, that she would ensure the safe delivery of infants of women who prayed to her before giving birth. At the same time she declared that anyone founding a church in her honor or burning lights to her would obtain anything useful that he or she desired—another reason for the rapid spread of her cult.

———— ✛ ————

RIGHT Margaret of Antioch's legend records that when Satan, in the form of a dragon, swallowed her, the monster's belly burst open and she was unharmed.

LEFT Nicholas of Myra, the patron saint of children (page 48) brings three murdered boys back to life.

Margaret of Antioch tramples on the dragon she has killed with a cross-tipped spear, symbolizing the victory of good over evil.

✛

Existence unlikely
FEAST DAY: 20 July in West (suppressed in 1969);
13 July in East
ALSO KNOWN AS: Marina (in Eastern church)
CULT: Early and widespread
OTHER PATRONAGES: Safe childbirth
ALSO INVOKED: For divine protection when
dying; escape from devils
EMBLEM: Dragon

✛

INFANTS
✛
NICHOLAS OF TOLENTINO
(1245–1305)

Nicholas was born in Ancona in the Marches of northern Italy. He was the first child of middle-aged parents and they named him after St. Nicholas of Myra, at whose tomb they had prayed for a son. His mother had promised that if her prayers were granted her son would faithfully serve God and Nicholas joined the Austin Friars in 1263, when he was 18. He was ordained seven years later and became famous as a healer and wonder-worker.

He moved from one friary to another until c. 1274, when a heavenly voice directed him to go to Tolentino. Sent there by the friars shortly afterwards, he was to remain there for the rest of his life. The town had suffered during the wars between the Guelphs, who

According to legend, in the months before his death Nicholas of Tolentino was soothed by angelic choirs who assured him of his salvation.

supported the pope against the Holy Roman Emperor, and their opponents, the Ghibellines. Civil disorder and immorality were rife and Nicholas was ordered to preach in the streets. His success in this and as a pastoral priest was spectacular.

For the next 30 years he tended Tolentino's destitute, ministered to criminals and mediated in quarrels and estrangements. Many miracles were attributed to him: he is said to have healed the sick by giving them pieces of "St. Nicholas' Bread" over which he had invoked the Virgin Mary's blessing. One of his particular devotions was to mothers and their newborn babies, hence his role as their patron.

He died on 10 September 1305, after a long illness; but although steps were immediately undertaken for his canonization, this did not come about until 1446.

1245 born Sant'Angelo, March of Ancona; 1263 joined Austin Friars; 1270 ordained; 1275 friary at Tolentino; 1305 died Tolentino; 1446 canonized
FEAST DAY: 10 September
CULT: Widespread in Europe and America.
Confined to local calendars since 1969
OTHER PATRONAGES: The dying;
souls in purgatory
EMBLEM: Basket containing bread rolls

BABIES
✦
ZENO OF VERONA
(died 371)

Zeno was born in Africa and, in 360, became bishop of Verona. A trained orator, he was famed as a preacher and the texts of 93 of his sermons have survived. During the 11 years of his episcopate he founded many churches and was zealous in countering heresy and developing Christian doctrine. His emblem is a fish, which a Veronese tradition explains as reflecting his love of angling, but which more probably represents his role as a savior of souls.

His patronage of babies is based on the legend that he was stolen at birth by the devil, who substituted a goblin in his place. Although the goblin suckled Zeno's mother for 18 years he never grew. Zeno, who had been reared by monks, was fortuitously summoned to investigate the phenomenon and made the goblin regurgitate all the milk into a great vat.

Born Africa; 362 bishop of Verona; 371 died Verona
FEAST DAY: 12 April
EMBLEM: Fish and fishing rod

Zeno was a celebrated preacher and zealous in performing his pastoral duties. In this fifteenth-century painting he is shown exorcizing the daughter of Emperor Gallienus.

CHILDREN

✢

NICHOLAS OF MYRA

(fourth century)

Nicholas—best known as Santa Claus—is one of the most popular of all the saints, but paradoxically very little is known of him as a man: the only certainty is that he was bishop of Myra (now Mugla in south-western Turkey) during the fourth century.

Legends about the saint are highly fanciful, but all attest to his loving kindness. He is said to have saved three girls from prostitution by providing three bags of gold for their dowries, to have saved from death three unjustly condemned men, to have rescued three sailors from drowning and—the most popular tale—to have brought to life three boys who were murdered by a butcher and hidden in a bran tub.

Many of his patronages spring from these stories, the most popular being his patronage of children. The longstanding tradition in the Low Countries of giving presents to children on his feast day—just one of many local customs which grew up as part of his cult—is the basis for his modern metamorphosis into Santa Claus. Dutch settlers in North America knew him as Sinte Klaas, a dialect version of his name, and merged legends about his generosity to children with Scandinavian folklore tales about a wizard who rewarded good children with presents; these became popular in the United States and then spread worldwide.

Before his transformation into Santa Claus, Nicholas of Myra was generally portrayed as he is here, wearing a bishop's robes and miter.

✢

Fourth century bishop of Myra
FEAST DAY: 6 December
CULT: Widespread from the eleventh century
when his relics were stolen from Myra and taken to
Bari in Italy
OTHER PATRONAGES: Sailors; unmarried girls;
merchants; pawnbrokers; apothecaries; Russia
EMBLEMS: Three balls; anchor; ship

✢

BOYS

✢

JOHN BOSCO

(1815–1888)

John was only two years old when his father, a Piedmontese peasant farmer, died. His early life was spent in extreme poverty—when he entered the seminary at Turin at the age of 16 his parish priest had to provide him with a cloak, the mayor gave him a hat and parishioners contributed his cassock and shoes.

He had recognized his vocation five years earlier when a dream made it clear to him that his duty was to help and educate poor youths. He remained true to this commitment for the rest of his life, the reason for his patronage of boys.

Don Cafasso, his teacher and religious guide, introduced him to benefactors who helped him in his work and John was appointed chaplain of a refuge for girls, a post that left him free to minister to young men on Sundays. He resigned this post and with his mother, "Mamma Margaret," opened a boarding house for about 40 neglected boys in the Valdocco suburb of Turin. Workshops in tailoring and shoemaking were established in 1853.

In 1859, with 22 companions, John started to organize the Salesian Order, called after St. Francis de Sales. It was approved by Pope Pius IX in 1874 and when John died in 1888 it had 768 members, with 26 houses in the Americas and 38 in Europe. Today, thousands of Salesians all over the world specialize in pastoral work and education. In 1872, John founded a similar order for nuns: the Daughters of Our Lady, Help of Christians.

John Bosco was a charismatic personality who handled difficult charges with gentle firmness. Well-attested miracles, including the multiplication of food, are attributed to him. He believed that boys born and brought up in cities benefited immeasurably from natural beauty and from music, and combined both in Sunday expeditions to the country that started with mass and included games and a picnic.

Forty thousand people visited John's body when it lay in state after his death in 1888, and much of the population of Turin followed his funeral. He was canonized in 1934, less than half a century after his death.

✛

1815 born Piedmont, Italy; 1831 entered seminary in Turin; 1841 ordained; 1859 organized Salesian Order; 1888 died Turin;
1934 canonized
FEAST DAY: 31 January
OTHER PATRONAGES: Editors; apprentices

✛

GIRLS

✛

MARIA GORETTI
(1890–1902)

Maria was born near Ancona, Italy, into a peasant family, and was a happy and cheerful girl who was at the same time devout and unselfish. When she was twelve years old, a local youth, Alexander Serenelli, attempted to rape her while her widowed mother was out at work. Maria resisted with all her strength and Alexander stabbed her; she died the next day. Alexander was imprisoned for many years, and in 1910 repented of his deed. Released in 1929, he was eventually reconciled with Maria's mother, and lived to see Maria's canonization in 1950. She is honored by the Church for preferring death to defilement, and is a pattern and model for young girls.

✛

1890 born Corinaldo near Ancona, Italy; 1902 murdered by Alexander Serenelli; 1950 canonized
FEAST DAY: July 6

✛

John Bosco died in 1888 but, as this allegory shows, he lives on in the institutes he founded.

TEENAGERS
✛
ALOYSIUS GONZAGA
(1568–1591)

Aloysius' early years were spent at the courts of Tuscany, Mantua and Spain. His mother, Marta, was a lady-in-waiting to Philip II of Spain's queen, and his father, Ferrante, marquis of Castiglione, was a member of a powerful and illustrious Lombard family.

Although the marquis's dearest wish was that Aloysius, his eldest son, should grow up to be a great soldier, the boy had no interest in a military career. He had been pious from early childhood and was increasingly attracted by a life of Christian devotion. He was about nine years old, and in attendance at the Florentine court of Francesco de Medici, when a painful kidney disease caused him to retire from public life and spend his time reading the Lives of the Saints. During his holidays from Florence he instructed the poor boys of Castiglione in the catechism. He also fasted three days a week, scourged himself with a whip and woke to pray at midnight even in bitterly cold weather.

Aloysius was appointed a page at the duke of Mantua's court in 1579 and then moved to the court of Don Diego of Spain from 1581 to 1583. Although he fulfilled his duties faithfully he was revolted by the corruption and licentiousness of noble society, and decided to become a Jesuit. Despite his family's protests he entered the order, in Rome, in 1585 at the age of 17. He was the ideal novice and became a full member of the Society of Jesus two years later. He contracted the plague in 1591, while nursing sufferers in the Jesuits' hospital, and died three months later from a lingering fever, at the age of 23. Because he is a model of pious youth he was declared the patron of young people in 1729, three years after his canonization.

✛

1568 born Castiglione, Lombardy; 1585 Jesuit
novice, Rome; 1587 accepted into the order; 1591
died Rome; 1621 cult approved at Rome;
1726 canonized
FEAST DAY: 21 June

✛

ORPHANS AND ABANDONED CHILDREN
✛
JEROME EMILIANI
(1481–1537)

As a young man Jerome was an officer in the Venetian army, at a time when the republic was at war with both Pope Julius II and Maximilian I, Holy Roman Emperor. His conversion came after he had been taken prisoner. While kept in chains in a dungeon he prayed to the Blessed Virgin Mary, and was miraculously set free.

Jerome was ordained in 1518, when he was 37, and devoted himself to relieving the famine and plague that were rife in northern Italy.

Orphans and abandoned children were a particular concern of his throughout his life, hence his patronage of them. He strongly believed in the value of education, and was a pioneer in using the catechism method to teach young children. When he himself caught, and recovered from, the plague in 1531 he gave thanks by establishing three orphanages.

He also founded a hospital and a house for repentant prostitutes. In the following year he established the Somaschi—named after their place or origin—a congregation of priests who received special training and whose principal work was to care for orphans.

Jerome was 56 when he died of an infectious disease caught while tending the sick.

✛

1481 born Venice; 1518 ordained; 1531 founded
orphanages at Brescia, Como, Bergamo
and house for repentant prostitutes
plus hospital at Verona; 1532 founded the
congregation of clerks, the Somaschi; 1537 died;
1540 congregation recognized by Pope Paul III;
1767 canonized; 1928 declared the patron of
orphans and abandoned children by Pope Pius XI
FEAST DAY: 8 February (formerly 20 July)
EMBLEM: Ball and chain

SCHOOLCHILDREN
+
BENEDICT
(c. 480–c. 550)

Benedict's "Holy Rule" has been the fundamental monastic code in Europe since the early Middle Ages, and was a potent factor in the development and flowering of Western civilization. Nevertheless, comparatively little is known about this most influential of monks. The only information comes from Pope Gregory the Great's *Dialogues*, which were written more than 40 years after Benedict's death and dwell extensively on the wonders he performed.

Benedict was born at Nursia in Umbria, Italy, and like his twin sister Scholastica—who founded the Benedictine order of nuns—was brought up as a staunch Christian. When he was 14 he went to Rome to study but, disturbed by the profligate life in a city that was rapidly descending into barbarism, and fearing that he might succumb to its temptations, he soon left to live an ascetic life in the mountains outside the city. In 500, at the age of about 20, he became a hermit in a cave near Subiaco. Over the next 30 years his sanctity attracted many disciples, whom he organized into 12 small monastic communities. However, there was also intense local jealousy, and even an attempt on his life in c. 525: he was offered a poisoned drink but is said to have rendered it harmless by blessing it.

In c. 530 Benedict left for Monte Cassino where he established a monastery and wrote the final version of his Rule. Characterized by moderation and obedience within the framework of a disciplined community life,

Benedict founded the Benedictines in the sixth century; today they are primarily a teaching order.

+

it was described by him as a "little rule for beginners": he saw it as an example rather than as the blueprint for the monastic life which it became. This is indicative of his modesty, which he combined with wisdom, discretion and loving kindness. His insistence on good discipline and respect for others made him the spiritual father of his community. He died in 547, supported by his disciples as he stood in prayer before the altar, and was buried in the same grave as his sister.

Benedict is the patron of schoolchildren because the Benedictine monks have run, through the centuries, important and often distinguished monastic schools.

Today the Benedictines are known primarily as a teaching order.

+

c. 480 born Nursia, Umbria; 494 went to Rome, became a hermit at Subiaco; c. 530 went to Monte Cassino; c. 550 died; sixth to tenth centuries Rule spread north of the Alps and in Italy
FEAST DAY: 11 July (formerly 21 March)
CULT: Spread with his Rule; the monasteries of Monte Cassino in Italy and Fleury (Saint-Benoît-sur-Loire) in France both claim his relics
OTHER PATRONAGES: Europe (since 1964); farmworkers; coppersmiths; the dying
ALSO INVOKED: Against poison; fever; gall-stones; nettle rash; poison; witchcraft
EMBLEMS: Raven; broken cup

+

RIGHT *Benedict
blesses St Maurus,
one of his pupils,
before the young
monk leaves on a
mission to teach in
France.*

BELOW *Benedict is
tempted by a vision
of a woman. To
repress his desire
for her he rolled
naked in nettles
and briars.*

RIGHT *Benedict and
his monks at a
refectory table, one
of a series of
sixteenth-century
frescoes depicting
scenes from the
saint's life.
Benedict's Rule, on
which Western
monasticism is
based, called for
poverty, chastity
and obedience.*

STUDENTS
✜
JEROME
(c. 341–420)

There are many contradictions in Jerome's life and character. He was brought up in Strido in Dalmatia by devout Christian parents, but was, unusually, over 18 before he was baptized. The classics—records of a pagan past—were his lifelong passion. He was ordained priest but believed that his true vocation was as a monk or recluse. And although he was loved by his friends and followers, idealistic, and considerate to the poor and sick, he was also short-tempered and cantankerous, sarcastic and insulting, and treated those who opposed his views with vituperative contempt.

✜

While in Rome Jerome instructed St. Paula and a group of Christian women in Scripture.

Jerome was in his late 20s and had already studied Latin and Greek in Rome, and traveled extensively in Gaul (now France), Italy and Dalmatia, before he fully embraced Christianity. He decided to become a monk and in c. 370 settled in Aquileia, near Venice, with a group of friends. The community was shortlived, however, and in 374 Jerome became a hermit in the Holy Land, in the desert near Antioch. Here he wrestled with the temptations of the flesh, and later learned Hebrew from a rabbi in order to read the scriptures in their original language. He accepted ordination with some reluctance in Antioch, and studied under St. Gregory Nazianen, one of the great Greek Doctors of the Church, in Constantinople. In 382 he returned to Rome where the aged and cultivated pope, St. Damasus, employed him as his secretary and commissioned him to write a standard Latin text of the Bible, now known as the Vulgate. This task occupied him for the next 22 years; the depth and breadth of scholarship and the application it required are the basis of his patronage of students.

While he continued in his great endeavor Jerome became the leader of a group of women whom he instructed in Christianity. However, his sojourn in Rome did not last long. Although the Romans were impressed by his honesty and holiness, Jerome was disliked for his sarcasm and irascibility. It seemed to many that his forceful advocacy of celibacy belittled the honor they felt was due to matrimony, and pagans were offended by his harsh condemnation of them. There was also scandalous, if unjustified, gossip about his relations with St. Paula, one of his followers.

In 385 Jerome returned to the Holy Land and, with Paula and her daughter St. Eustochium, who had followed him, settled at Bethlehem where he founded a community of monks and nuns. He spent the rest of his life teaching, studying and writing. Paula died in 404 and, after the sacking of Rome in 410, Jerome's retreat was disturbed by refugees from the city and raids by the Huns. He was also persecuted by the Pelagians, a heretical Christian sect, who assaulted his followers and set fire to the monasteries.

The most learned biblical scholar of his day, and one of the four great Doctors of the Church, Jerome died in 420 at the age of 79. He was buried in the Church of the Nativity at Bethlehem, next to Paula and her daughter Eustochium.

---

c. 341 born Strido, Dalmatia; 366 baptized; 370 monk at Aquileia; 374 hermit near Antioch; 379 ordained; 382 Rome; 385 Bethlehem; 420 died Bethlehem; relics translated to Rome
FEAST DAY: 30 September
ALSO KNOWN AS: Eusebius Hieronymus Sophronius (Roman name)
EMBLEMS: Lion; cardinal's hat

SICK CHILDREN
BEUNO
(died c. 640)

All that is known of Beuno is that he was an abbot in North Wales, that he founded monasteries in Wales and Herefordshire, and that he died at his chief foundation, Clynnog Fawr in Gwynedd, and was buried there.

His patronage of sick children is based on a legend that makes him St. Winifred's uncle. According to this tradition, Caradoc, a chieftain's son, was so infuriated when Winifred repulsed his attentions that he beheaded her with his sword. The earth opened up and swallowed him and Beuno replaced his niece's head on her shoulders and so brought her back to life.

The legend is an enduring one: as late as the eighteenth century sick children were bathed in Beuno's holy well and left overnight in his tomb.

---

c. 640 died
FEAST DAY: 21 April

STAMMERING CHILDREN
NOTKAR BALBULUS
(c. 840–912)

Born in 840 at Heiligau (now Elgg) near St. Gall, Switzerland, Notkar entered the novitiate at St. Gall when still a child, and grew up to become a monk, an exemplary priest, a fine poet, musician and teacher—as well as being noted for his modesty. He held the offices of guest-master, librarian and precentor of his abbey, and his talents encompassed the writing of liturgies, hymns, a martyrology, hagiography and poetry. Because of a missing tooth and speech defect he was known as Notkar Balbulus, the Stammerer, from which arose his patronage of those people, particularly children, similarly affected.

---

c. 840 born Elgg, Switzerland; 912 died St. Gall
FEAST DAY: 7 May (formerly 6 April)
CULT: Centered on St. Gall; confirmed by Pope Julius II in 1512
OTHER PATRONAGE: Musicians
EMBLEMS: Book; staff

CHAPTER FOUR

✛

INDOOR PROFESSIONS

Happy is the man that findeth wisdom.

PROVERBS 3:13

─────────── ✛ ───────────

ACADEMICS

─────────── ✛ ───────────

THOMAS AQUINAS
(1225–1274)

Regarded by many historians as the most outstand-ing thinker and theologian of the Middle Ages, Thomas was the youngest son of Landulf, count of Aquino near Naples. He was always destined for high ecclesiastical office and was sent to school at the Benedictine monastery of Monte Cassino at the age of five. He later spent five years at the University of Naples where, in c.1244, he secretly joined the Do-minican friars, a new order that was dependent on alms for sustenance. This so outraged his aristocratic relations that they had him kidnapped and imprisoned for over a year. They made every effort to force him to renounce his vows: on one occasion they brought a beautiful prostitute to his room but Thomas chased her away with a flaming torch. From that day he was free from sexual desire—although a biographer records that "he always shunned women . . . as a man avoids snakes." Thomas' family eventually relented and in 1248 he went to Paris and Cologne to study under Albert the Great.

Massively built, slow-moving and amiably taciturn,

─────────── ✛ ───────────

LEFT *An early Byzantine ikon of Gabriel, patron saint of diplomats (page 59) and Michael, special protector of grocers and supermarket workers (page 71).*

Thomas Aquinas combined teaching and preaching with writing. The Summa Theologica, *his greatest work, profoundly influenced Christian thought.*

─────────── ✛ ───────────

he was nicknamed "the dumb ox" by his fellow stu-dents. When he did speak he was so brilliant that Albert prophesied: "This dumb ox will fill the world with his bellowing." In 1252 he went to teach theo-logy at the University of Paris, then the intellectual powerhouse of Europe.

Thomas received his mastership of theology in Paris

ABOVE Thomas Aquinas in the robes of a Dominican friar; the dove at his ear symbolizes divine inspiration

RIGHT Slow moving and taciturn, Thomas Aquinas was nicknamed the "dumb ox" by fellow students at Cologne; he was nevertheless a brilliant lecturer.

in 1256 and, after teaching at the university for three years, spent the next decade working in Italy. Already greatly admired for his theological works including the *Summa contra Gentes*, he started his greatest work, the *Summa Theologica*, in about 1266, but left it unfinished when, in December 1273, he experienced a mysterious vision while saying mass. After that he refused to write another word, declaring that what he had written seemed like straw compared with what he had seen. Three months later he died.

Even in its incomplete state the *Summa Theologica* runs to over two million words and exemplifies Thomas' industry: he was even said to compose Latin prose in his sleep.

The devotion with which he served God through scholarship, in this and his other works, is the reason for his patronage of academics. He was canonized in 1323, 50 years after his death.

---✝---

1225 born Roccasecca near Aquino, Naples; 1230 entered Benedictine monastery at Monte Cassino; c. 1244 joined Dominicans; 1248 Universities of Paris and Cologne; 1256 received mastership of theology at Paris; 1261 Orvieto; 1268 Viterbo; 1269 Paris; 1272 Naples; 1274 died Fossanuova near Terracina; 1323 canonized; 1368 relics translated to Saint-Sernin, Toulouse; 1567 declared a Doctor of the Church
FEAST DAY: 28 January (formerly 7 March)
OTHER PATRONAGES: Roman Catholic schools, colleges, universities; booksellers; philosophers; theologians; pencil makers
ALSO INVOKED: For chastity; learning. Against storms; lightning
EMBLEMS: Star; chalice; ox; monstrance

---✝---

DIPLOMATS
✛
GABRIEL THE ARCHANGEL

The archangel Gabriel appears four times in the Bible, always as the messenger of God, hence his patronage of diplomats who are, like him, the bearers of messages.

In the Old Testament he interprets Daniel's visions and announces the time of the coming of the Messiah to him. In the New Testament he foretells to Zacharias the birth of his son John the Baptist. But Gabriel's principal role is as God's ambassador to Mary: "...thou shalt conceive in thy womb, and bring forth a son, and shall call his name Jesus."

✛

FEAST DAY: 29 September (formerly 24 March)
CULT: Evident in early Christian Rome and throughout early Christian world; first invoked in the seventh century
OTHER PATRONAGES: Telecommunications; television; radio; postal services; stamp collectors
EMBLEMS: Spear; shield; lily

✛

Gabriel was worshiped as the herald of the Annunciation.

According to angelic lore, Gabriel was the governor of Eden and, in this role, has been identified with the angel in portrayals of Adam and Eve's expulsion. The bronze plaque (left) shows a winged being guarding the tree of life. The relief (above) shows Gabriel looking down on scenes from the Old Testament: Daniel in the lions' den, and Adam and Eve.

ABOVE *In art Gabriel is best known as the angel of the Annunciation. The lily he carries in this painting by Dante Gabriel Rossetti is a symbol of purity.*

RIGHT *Gabriel is generally shown with wings, as in this detail from an Annunciation by Fra Angelico.*

RIGHT *In Leonardo da Vinci's painting Mary is sitting in a garden when Gabriel appears to her; outdoor settings were common in Italian Renaissance art.*

ABOVE *In this painting by Fra Angelico, the Virgin Mary's cloak is blue—symbolizing heaven— and God the Father looks down on the scene. The Annunciation has always been a popular theme with painters, reflecting its importance in Christian doctrine.*

ABOVE *Gabriel holds a scepter—his emblem—in a detail from an altarpiece by Matthias Grünewald.*

ABOVE *El Greco's Annunciation shows the Virgin Mary reading a book— traditionally the Bible—and the Holy Spirit in the form of a dove. Gabriel stands on a cloud, suggesting his descent from heaven.*

TEACHERS OF BOYS
✛
JOHN-BAPTIST DE LA SALLE
(1651–1719)

John-Baptist's profound influence in the field of education makes him a natural choice as the patron saint of schoolteachers, particularly teachers of boys. He was admitted to minor orders at the age of 11, became a canon of Reims cathedral when only 16, and at first seemed destined for a life of ease and high ecclesiastical office. However, not long after his ordination in 1678 he resigned as a canon, gave away his fortune to help relieve famine in Champagne and dedicated himself to his life's work: the education of poor boys through devoted and loving teaching.

He opened four schools in the years following his ordination and in 1686 founded his congregation, the Brothers of the Christian Schools, in Reims, to train teachers in his methods. Then, as now, they were laymen, not priests. John-Baptist established two more training colleges in Paris and Saint-Denis in the teeth of fierce criticism from professional schoolmasters—and even the Church. Some critics objected to his revolutionary methods, which included teaching in the mother tongue rather than in Latin and in classes rather than individual tuition. Others believed that poor boys should be taught only manual skills.

Before his death, in 1719, John-Baptist had also set up a school for boys in the entourage of the exiled King James II of England, had opened a school in Rome and started Sunday schools in Paris, and had established a reformatory for disturbed youths. Today there are some 20,000 "Christian Brothers" worldwide, in establishments that range from primary schools and university colleges to approved schools.

✛

1651 born Reims; 1667 canon of Reims cathedral; 1678 ordained; 1679 first two schools established; 1686 Brothers of the Christian Schools founded; 1695 drew up his Rule, *The Conduct of Christian Schools*; 1702 escaped attempt to oust him as leader of his order; 1717 resigned; 1719 died Rouen; 1900 canonized; 1937 relics translated to Rome
FEAST DAY: 7 April

✛

TEACHERS OF GIRLS
✛
URSULA AND HER COMPANIONS
(c. fourth century)

The fanciful legends that surround Ursula agree on only a few points: that she was a convinced virgin, the daughter of a British king; and that she was martyred in Cologne by invading Huns because she was a Christian and because she refused to marry their king.

One tradition further describes how, on her betrothal to a pagan prince, she demanded three years' grace before the marriage itself—a period she spent sailing to the mouth of the Rhine, to Cologne and Basle, and then on a pilgrimage to Rome, before

John-Baptist de la Salle was responsible for introducing many revolutionary teaching methods.

This fifteenth-century portrayal of Ursula shows her sheltering her companions under her cloak. In her right hand she holds the arrow that killed her.

returning to Cologne. She was accompanied on her travels by ten noble companions, each on a ship that carried one thousand virgins. According to another version of the tale, Ursula demanded, and received, as the price of marriage to a suitor, that he should provide ships and ten thousand virgin companions, to carry her on a pilgrimage that took her to Rome and then on to Cologne. Here she and her companions were overtaken by an invading horde of Huns who made sexual advances to them. Ursula, their preceptress, told them to die rather than submit—the basis for her patronage of girls and their instructresses.

Underlying these legends is a Latin inscription, cut into stone in about 400, and recording the rebuilding of a church at Cologne in memory of some anonymous

virgin martyrs. By the late ninth century the name of Ursula was attached to one of a group of up to eleven virgin martyrs; a century later—probably as the result of a misreading of a Latin text—their number had multiplied to 11,000.

✦

c. Fourth century
FEAST DAY: 21 October
CULT: Spread in Germany, Italy and the Low Countries after 1155 when a great collection of bones was discovered at Cologne and attributed to Ursula and her 11,000 virgin companions; reduced to local status 1969
EMBLEMS: Arrow; clock; ship

✦

PHILOSOPHERS
✦
JUSTIN
(c. 100–165)

The first Christian philosopher, Justin was born in Palestine to pagan Greek parents and studied the works of the Stoics, Pythagoreans and Platonists, before becoming a Christian when he was in his early 30s. He remained a layman and a philosopher, and as he traveled spreading the gospel in many lands he continued to hold disputations with Jews, pagans and heretics—the basis of his patronage of philosophers.

Justin's public argument with a Cynic in Rome was the probable reason for his arrest and subsequent decapitation with six other Christians. A record of his trial, during which he confessed his Christianity and refused to sacrifice to pagan gods, has been preserved. His *Apologies for the Christian Religion* and *Dialogue with the Jew Trypho* are valuable and instructive.

✦

c. 100 born Nablus, Palestine; c. 130 conversion to Christianity; c. 150 first visit to Rome;
165 martyred at Rome
FEAST DAY: 1 June
OTHER PATRONAGE: Apologists
EMBLEMS: Ax; sword; pen

✦

THEOLOGIANS
✛
AUGUSTINE OF HIPPO
(354–430)

Augustine is probably best known for the contrast between his dedication to Christianity in his later years and his earlier self-indulgence, summed up in his prayer: "Give me chastity and continence, but not yet."

The son of a pagan father and a Christian mother, St. Monica, he was born in Tagaste in North Africa (Algeria). His first ambition was to be a lawyer and he studied rhetoric at the University of Carthage, meanwhile living openly with a mistress for 14 years from the age of 16. Their son, Adeodatus, a future saint, was always cherished by his father. At this stage in his life Augustine was attracted by Manicheism, a heretical doctrine based on the conflict between good and evil, light and darkness.

Still in search of a philosophy, he taught rhetoric, first at Carthage, Tagaste and Rome and then, from 384, in Milan. Here he was influenced by the eloquence and teachings of the city's bishop, St. Ambrose, and after agonizing over the choice between a secular life that would bring him wealth and the comforts of marriage and an ascetic one of hardship and dedication, he was baptized, with his son, in 386.

He left for Africa and after spending a few years in a small monastic community near Tagaste he was ordained in 391. Augustine was appointed bishop of Hippo in 394 and, for the rest of his life, devoted his enormous energy and brilliant intellect to defending the Christian faith and refuting the many heresies that were current at the time—the reason for his patronage of theologians.

The Vandals were at the gates of Hippo when he died. Nevertheless his works, which include two of the world's classics—the *Confessions* and the *City of God*—survived the barbarism that followed; and the ideas on the religious life attributed to this most prolific and influential Doctor of the Church have been followed for many centuries by the Augustinian order of canons named after him.

Botticelli's fresco of Augustine of Hippo shows him in his cell. Although the Augustinian Order was only established six centuries after the saint's death, many artists have portrayed him at a desk writing his Rule.

✛

354 born Tagaste, Algeria; 370 University of Carthage; 383 taught rhetoric at Carthage, Tagaste, Rome; 384 Milan; 386 baptized and returned to Africa; 388 monastic community near Tagaste; 391 ordained; 394 bishop of Hippo; c. 400 *Confessions*; c. 412 *City of God*; 430 died Hippo
FEAST DAY: 28 August
CULT: Early and widespread
OTHER PATRONAGES: Brewers; printers
ALSO INVOKED: Against sore eyes
EMBLEMS: Pastoral staff; heart of fire

✛

Both these illustrations depict Matthew with a book, the attribute of the writer. On the left, the former tax collector holds his gospel under his arm. In the painting below a winged being is dictating to him.

ACCOUNTANTS
✛
MATTHEW
(first century)

Traditionally the author of the first Gospel, Matthew was originally called Levi but took his new name, meaning "the gift of Yahweh," when Jesus called him to be a disciple.

Until then he had been a tax collector for the Romans—a profession detested by Jews and Gentiles alike, and the basis of his patronage of bankers and accountants. After the Ascension he is said to have preached Christianity to his fellow Jews and was eventually martyred in Ethiopia or Persia.

✛

First century
FEAST DAY: 21 September
OTHER PATRONAGES: Tax collectors; customs officers; security guards
EMBLEMS: Inkwell; spear, sword or halberd; money bag or money box

✛

LAWYERS
✦
IVO
(1253–1303)

The son of a Breton landowner, Ivo studied law at Paris and Orléans and practiced in both civil and ecclesiastical courts in his native Brittany with success and probity—the basis of his patronage of lawyers. He defended the poverty-stricken and destitute as well as the rich and soon became known as "the Advocate of the Poor." He was not yet 30 when he was appointed diocesan judge, first in Rennes and then in Tréguier. In this office he was known for being fairminded, incorruptible and always concerned to defend the interests of the poor.

An ascetic since his student days, Ivo was ordained priest in 1284. Although he devoted himself entirely to parochial work from 1287, his knowledge of the law—like his time and possessions—was always available to his parishioners. He died in 1303 and was canonized less than 50 years later.

———————— ✦ ————————

1253 born Kermartin near Tréguier, Brittany; 1284 ordained; 1303 died Louannec, Brittany; 1347 canonized
FEAST DAY: 19 May
ALSO KNOWN AS: Yves; Yvo
OTHER PATRONAGES: Abandoned children; Brittany

———————— ✦ ————————

BUSINESS PEOPLE
✦
HOMOBONUS
(died 1197)

Homobonus, a merchant of Cremona in Italy, was a layman who was recognized as a saint at a time when canonization was normally bestowed only on bishops, monks, martyrs or kings. Prophetically named at his baptism—Homobonus means "good man"—he believed that his business, which he inherited from his father, was employment given to him by God. This belief, the scrupulous honesty with which he practiced his trade as well as his conspicuous charity to the poor—he gave away a large proportion of his profits—are the reasons for his patronage of business people.

Throughout his life Homobonus attended his parish church both in the mornings and in the evenings. He died during mass while prostrated in the form of a cross. His canonization, at the urgent request of his fellow citizens, was granted just two years after his death.

———————— ✦ ————————

1197 died Cremona, Italy
FEAST DAY: 13 November
OTHER PATRONAGES: Tailors; clothworkers

———————— ✦ ————————

SCIENTISTS
✦
ALBERT THE GREAT
(1206–1280)

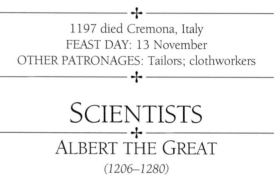

Although Albert the Great rose to become a bishop, his true vocation was that of teacher and scholar. The son of the count of Böllstadt, he first attended Padua University where, at the age of 17 and much against the wishes of his family, he joined the Dominicans. The order later sent him to the University of Paris to study and teach, and in 1244 he gained his master's degree in theology. From 1248 to 1252 he was director of studies at Cologne where his pupils included St. Thomas Aquinas. In 1260 Albert accepted the see of Regensburg. However, he resigned his bishopric after two years believing that he was more useful as a teacher, and retired to Cologne. Here he taught and wrote for most of the next 18 years until, in 1278, his memory and then his mind failed. He died two years later.

Albert's printed works fill 38 volumes and are impressively wide-ranging, covering subjects as diverse as astronomy and botany, chemistry and geography, physics and geology. He also made extensive use of Aristotle's philosophical ideas in the context of

Albertus magnus
cum discipulis suis

ALBERTVS MAGNVS EPISCOP RATISPONE.

ABOVE *Albert the Great was known as the "Universal Doctor" because of his wide-ranging scholarship. He had a scientific interest in nature, and his writing included treatises on biology and physiology.*

ABOVE *Albert the Great was first and foremost a teacher; his pupils included St. Thomas Aquinas, whose writings he defended against attack in 1277.*

✣

theology, work which St. Thomas Aquinas was to build on. Beatified in 1622, he was canonized in 1931 and was declared by Pope Pius XI to be the patron saint of scientists, because he possessed, in the highest degree, "that rare and divine gift, scientific instinct."

✣

1206 born Böllstadt; 1223 entered Dominican order; 1244 gained master's degree in theology; 1248–52 director of studies at Cologne; 1254 appointed prior-provincial of his order in Germany; 1260–62 bishop of Regensburg; 1263 retired to Cologne; 1280 died; 1622 beatified; 1931 canonized
FEAST DAY: 15 November

✣

ENGINEERS
✢
FERDINAND III OF CASTILE
(1198–1252)

A warrior king who became ruler of Castile when only about 19 years old, Ferdinand was well-connected to Europe's ruling families: his mother was a granddaughter of Henry II of England; St. Louis of France was a cousin; his first father-in-law was Philip of Swabia, Holy Roman Emperor; and his own daughter, Eleanor, married the future Edward I of England.

Unlike most of his contemporaries, Ferdinand did not wage war to extend his own territories. Rather, his object was to recapture land that his Spanish kingdom had lost to the Moors. His campaign lasted for 27 years but was ultimately successful: most of Andalusia was recovered from its oppressors.

Ferdinand was a wise and tolerant ruler, who said that he "feared more the curse of one old woman than the whole army of the Moors," and who administered justice severely but impartially. He became king of Castile in 1217 and united it with León, which he inherited in 1230. He founded the University of Salamanca and, in thanksgiving for his victories, rebuilt Burgos cathedral and converted a Seville mosque into a church. In Castile he is best remembered for his victories over the Moors and for the technical military skills that are the basis of his patronage of engineers.

He died in 1252 and was buried in Seville cathedral wearing the robes of a friar. Although his people immediately acclaimed him as a saint, it was 400 years before he was canonized.

✢

1198 born near Salamanca; 1217 king of Castile;
1219 married Beatrice, daughter of Philip of Swabia;
1230 became king of León; 1237 married Joan of
Ponthieu; 1252 died Seville; 1671 canonized
FEAST DAY: 30 May
CULT: Immediate and widespread
OTHER PATRONAGES: Rulers; governors;
magistrates; the poor; prisoners; Seville
EMBLEM: Greyhound

✢

DENTISTS
✢
APOLLONIA
(died 249)

A pollonia, described as a "marvelous aged virgin" by her contemporary St. Denis, died when the heathen population of Alexandria rioted against the Christians. Denis, the city's bishop, records that she was struck repeatedly in the face until all her teeth were broken. The mob then lit a bonfire and threatened to burn her if she did not renounce her faith. Apollonia said a short prayer and walked into the fire of her own accord, "being kindled within by the greater fire of the holy spirit." Later legend makes her a beautiful girl whose teeth were extracted with pincers, hence her patronage of dentists.

✢
---

249 died Alexandria
FEAST DAY: 9 February
CULT: Became popular in Western church; reduced
to local status in 1970
ALSO INVOKED: Against toothache
EMBLEM: Pincers gripping tooth

✢

ABOVE Apollonia is traditionally painted as a young woman and often holds a tooth in a forceps.

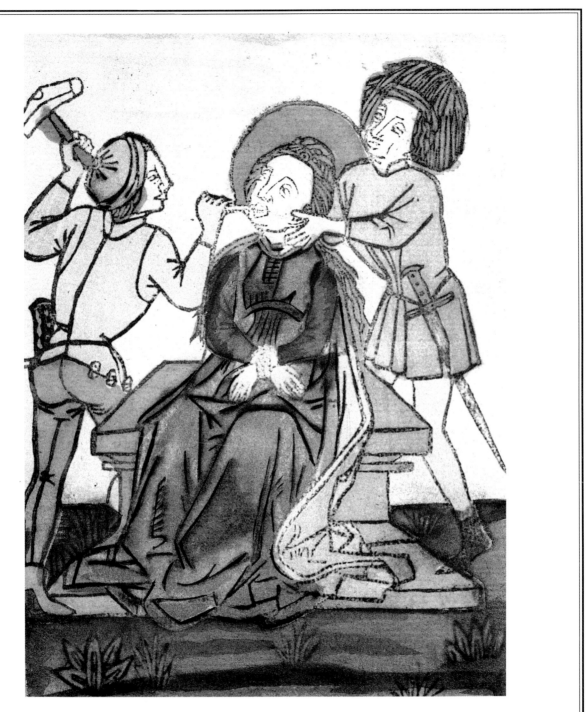

ABOVE *Apollonia's torture; it is said that before she died*
she promised to help sufferers from toothache.

DOCTORS
✣
COSMAS AND DAMIAN
(date unknown)

The legends surrounding Cosmas and Damian are built on the barest of facts: that two men with their names were martyred in Cyrrhus, in Syria, and that a basilica was built in their honor. Tradition makes them twin Arab brothers, both skilled physicians, who were professed Christians and who came to be known as the "holy moneyless ones" because they refused payment from their patients. This practical charity, and the many miraculous cures attributed to them, are the reasons for their patronage of doctors.

One curious legend describes how the brothers amputated a man's leg and replaced it with the leg of a Moor. The patient recovered but found that he now had one white leg and one brown one.

Cosmas and Damian were martyred by being beheaded, but not before other methods of execution had been tried. They were drowned, but angels saved them. They were burned, but fire failed to harm them. And they were stoned, but the stones turned round and hit those who had thrown them.

✣

Date unknown
FEAST DAY: 26 September
CULT: Centered at Cyrrhus, Syria; relics brought to Rome and cult spread through the Christian world; popular during Middle Ages
OTHER PATRONAGES: Surgeons; pharmacists; barbers; hairdressers
ALSO INVOKED: Against hernias; pestilence
EMBLEMS: Box of ointment; phial

✣ ──────────── ✣ ────────────

Numerous healing miracles were attributed to Cosmas and Damian after their death; in particular, it was said that they appeared to sick people while they slept—and cured them before they woke.

Cosmas and Damian are here holding palm fronds— symbols of their martyrdom. They were patrons of the Medici family in Florence and especially popular during the Renaissance.

GROCERS AND SUPERMARKET WORKERS
✛
MICHAEL THE ARCHANGEL

O ne of the three angels who stand before the throne of God, Michael is described in the Book of Revelation as the leader of the victorious heavenly armies in their battle against Satan and his forces. God sent him to cast out Lucifer who led a rebellion among the angels, and he is generally identified with the Old Testament "angel of the Lord," the protector of Israel.

Michael is also the angel who receives risen souls and weighs them in the balance—the basis of his patronage of grocers.

Many visions of him have been seen, the first on Monte Gargano in Italy in the fifth century. An appearance in the eighth century led to the foundation of Mont-Saint-Michel Abbey in Normandy.

✛

FEAST DAY: 29 September (now with Gabriel and Raphael)
CULT: Began in East; spread to West from the fifth century
OTHER PATRONAGES: Battle; security forces; paratroopers; radiologists and radiotherapists; the dying
EMBLEMS: Scales; dragon; sword

✛

The Benedictine Abbey of Mont-Saint-Michel was founded in the tenth century, 200 years after Michael had appeared to St. Aubert and ordered him to build a church where the abbey now stands.

ABOVE Michael probably originated as an ancient Persian god of light, locked in eternal conflict with the forces of evil. He later became the protector of Israel, and eventually Christianity's "great captain"—the leading saint of the Church militant. Today his cult is worldwide; this statue is carried in Easter processions in Goa, India.

LEFT This Italian Renaissance painting shows the emblems that are traditionally associated with Michael: he carries a sword in one hand and a pair of scales in the other. Under his feet is a dragon, representing Satan.

SURGEONS
✦
LAMBERT OF MAASTRICHT
(c. 635–c. 705)

Lambert was born into a noble family in Maastricht (now in the Netherlands) and educated by the local bishop, Théodard. When his tutor was murdered in 670 Lambert was chosen as his successor and, as bishop, was active in supporting the missions of St. Willibrord and others against pagan cults. Because of his opposition to Elbroin, the influential and tyrannical mayor of the palace, Lambert was exiled for seven years to the Benedictine monastery of Stavelot (now in Belgium) where he continued his evangelical work. Elbroin was assassinated in 681 and his successor, Pepin of Herstal, restored Lambert to his see.

Lambert refuses to bless a cup offered by Alpais, believing that she was committing adultery with Pepin, her brother-in-law.

Lambert was murdered at the then tiny village of Liège in c. 705; he was said to have been pierced by a javelin, from which his patronage of surgeons arose. According to later legend, he died because he reproved Pepin for an adulterous liaison with his sister-in-law, but the real cause was probably a blood feud. He was soon recognized as a martyr.

✦

c. 635 born Maastricht; 670 bishop of Maastricht; 675–82 in exile at the monastery of Stavelot, Belgium; c. 705 murdered at Liège
FEAST DAY: 17 September
CULT: Centered on Liège where a substantial city grew up around the church built to house Lambert's relics
EMBLEM: Javelin or lance

✦

NURSES
✦
CAMILLUS DE LELLIS
(1550–1614)

Unusually tall and strong, Camillus spent his early years from the age of 17 as a mercenary in the Venetian army. During this time he was notoriously short-tempered and so addicted to gambling that he lost all his possessions—including, literally, his shirt which his creditors stripped off his back—and was ultimately forced to work as a laborer. All this changed soon after his 25th birthday when he heard a sermon that caused him to fall on his knees, deploring his past life and begging heaven for mercy.

He twice tried to join the Franciscans but could not be admitted to the order because of an incurable disease of the leg. This disability, which remained with him for the rest of his life, drew his attention to the sufferings of other people and he joined the hospital of San Giacomo in Rome, eventually becoming its bursar. He soon realized that the medical treatment there was inadequate and often brutal and, in 1585, a year after his ordination as a priest, he founded the Ministers of the Sick to care for people at home and in hospital. Members of this congregation also served with troops fighting in Hungary and Croatia in 1595 and 1601—the first recorded military nursing units.

Camillus pioneered what is now accepted nursing practice—fresh air, isolation of infectious patients and suitable diets—and before his death at the age of 64 he had founded 15 religious houses and eight hospitals. He was canonized in 1746 and in 1930 was proclaimed the patron saint of nurses.

1550 born Bocchianico in the Abruzzi (Italy); 1567 joined Venetian army; 1575 conversion; 1584 ordained priest; 1585 founded Ministers of the Sick in Rome; 1588 founded religious house in Naples; 1607 resigned leadership of order; 1614 died Genoa; 1746 canonized
FEAST DAY: 14 July

HEALERS
BRIDGET OF SWEDEN
(1303–1373)

The daughter of a Swedish nobleman, Bridget married a wealthy prince, Ulf Gudmarrson, when she was 14 years old and he was only 18. They lived happily together for the next 28 years and Bridget bore her husband eight children—one, Catherine, was also to be venerated as a saint. In 1335 Bridget was summoned to be principal lady-in-waiting to Blanche of Namur, the newly wedded wife of King Magnus II of Sweden, and began to experience a series of visions and revelations which made her an object of ridicule and did nothing to reform the lax moral standards of the court. Bridget retired to a Cistercian monastery after her husband's death in 1344, and two years later founded the monastery of Vadstena with the help of King Magnus. A mixed house for monks and nuns, it became the center of the Bridgettine order.

Bridget traveled to Rome in 1349 to seek confirmation of her order and remained there for the rest of her life. She never returned to Sweden. She offered advice—often outspoken—to the popes and cared for the poor and needy. Her work with the sick is the basis for her patronage of healers. She recorded her visions and prophecies in her controversial but widely influential book of Revelations; some contemporary theologians declared her to have been deceived. Nevertheless she was canonized 18 years after her death, and at its height in the later Middle Ages her order numbered 70 houses.

1303 born Sweden; 1317 married Ulf Gudmarrson; 1335 went to the court of Magnus II of Sweden; 1344 Ulf died; 1343–6 lived at the Cistercian monastery of Alvastra; 1346 founded monastery at Vadstena; 1349 went to Rome; 1373 died Rome; 1381 canonized
FEAST DAY: 23 July (formerly 8 October)
ALSO KNOWN AS: Birgitta; Birgit
EMBLEMS: Book; pilgrim's staff; heart and cross

FLORISTS
ROSE OF LIMA
(1586–1617)

The first canonized saint of the Americas was born Isabel de Flores y del Oliva, in Lima, Peru, but was always known as Rose. Her family was impoverished because of unsuccessful speculations in the mines, and as a young girl she supported her parents by growing flowers and by doing embroidery and other needlework. She refused even to consider marriage and, fearing that her beauty might be a source of temptation, rubbed her face with pepper to make her skin blotchy and her hands with lime to harden them.

When she was 20 she took a vow of virginity, joined the Third Order of St. Dominic, and retired to a summerhouse in her parents' garden. She wore a circlet studded with sharp prickles—a "crown of thorns"—and lived almost as a recluse. She spent many hours praying, underwent temptations and had mystical experiences that resulted in an ecclesiastical enquiry. She was also persecuted by her friends and others who disapproved of her way of life. Nevertheless she cared for the poor, slaves and the native population. Rose was 31 when she died after a long and painful illness. Her patronage of florists comes from her name, her early work as a grower of flowers, and the fact that she lived in, and loved and tended, her parents' garden.

---✣---

1586 born Lima, Peru; 1606 joined Dominicans;
1617 died Lima; 1671 canonized
FEAST DAY: 23 August
OTHER PATRONAGES: Gardeners; Peru;
Central and South America;
the Philippines; India
EMBLEMS: Roses; the Holy Infant

---✣---

BREWERS
✣
WENCESLAS
(907–929)

The "Good King Wenceslas" of the Christmas carol is a nineteenth-century fiction. The theme of the song springs from its composer's imagination; and the real Wenceslas was a duke, not a king.

The elder son of Duke Bratislav of Bohemia, Wenceslas was educated by his grandmother Ludmilla, a devoted Christian whose influence over him apparently led to her assassination in 921. When Wenceslas succeeded to the dukedom a year later, at the age of 15, he promoted Christianity and recognized a Christian king, Henry I of Germany, as his overlord—policies that enraged pagan members of Bohemia's nobility. Boleslaus, Wenceslas' younger brother, joined the malcontents and in 929 his supporters murdered the 22-year-old duke.

Wenceslas was proclaimed patron saint of Bohemia less than 30 years after his death and is now the symbol of Czech nationalism and independence. The country is renowned for its beer and, as its most notable saint, Wenceslas became patron of brewers.

---✣---

907 born near Prague; 922 duke of Bohemia;
926 recognized Henry I of Germany as his overlord;
929 died Stara Boleslaw

FEAST DAY: 28 September
ALSO KNOWN AS: Vaclav; Wenzel
CULT: Feast day celebrated in
Bohemia from 985
OTHER PATRONAGES: The Czech Republic;
Bohemia; Moravia
EMBLEMS: Banner; eagle; staff

---✣---

PUBLICANS
✣
JULIAN THE HOSPITALLER
(fictitious)

An entirely fictitious saint, Julian is, rather, the hero of a romance. This describes him as a nobleman who, while out hunting, was told by a hart that he would kill his father and mother. To avoid committing this terrible crime Julian traveled to a far country where he met, and married, a rich widow. The hart's prophecy came true when his parents came in search of him. He was away from home and his wife gave them her bed to sleep in. When Julian returned he found a man and woman asleep together and, believing that his wife was committing adultery, killed them.

In penance, he and his wife built a refuge for the poor by the side of a river. Here they cared for travelers—the reason for Julian's patronage of innkeepers and publicans—rowed them across the river and tended them when they were sick. One day they nursed a man, apparently a leper, who was half-dead with cold, placing him in their bed for warmth. The man died but as he went to heaven he told Julian that God had accepted his penance. Both Julian and his wife died soon afterwards.

---✣---

Fictitious
FEAST DAY: 12 February
ALSO KNOWN AS: Julian the Poor
CULT: Popular from the thirteenth century in
France, Flanders and England
OTHER PATRONAGES: Boatmen; travelers
EMBLEMS: Hart; oar

---✣---

*Julian devoted himself to caring for travelers, to atone
for killing his parents; his wife joined him in his penance.*

CHAPTER FIVE

✛

OUTDOOR PURSUITS

Therefore shall the strong people glorify thee ...
ISAIAH 25:3

✛

GARDENERS

✛

FIACRE
(died c. 670)

Fiacre was a misogynistic Irish hermit who left his homeland in search of greater solitude in France. St. Faro, bishop of Meaux, gave him land for a hermitage in nearby Breuil and here Fiacre created a garden; instead of using a plough he turned the soil with his staff, and unaided he cleared the ground of trees and weeds. His skill as a horticulturalist is the reason he is the patron saint of gardeners.

Fiacre attracted many disciples. He also established a hospice where he sometimes miraculously cured those who were sick. His healing miracles continued after his death. His association with French hackney carriages is an accident: when cabs first appeared for hire in Paris, in 1620, they were known as *fiacres* because their stand was near the Hotel Saint-Fiacre.

✛

c. 670 died
FEAST DAY: 30 August
CULT: Mainly in France, where it flourished
particularly during the seventeenth and eighteenth
centuries; Ireland from the twelfth century
OTHER PATRONAGES: Hosiers; cab drivers
ALSO INVOKED: Against haemorrhoids.
By sufferers from venereal disease
EMBLEM: Spade

✛

ABOVE One of Fiacre's legends records that he was of royal birth, and that he refused his ancestral crown, preferring solitude to worldly greatness.

LEFT A seventeenth-century Bulgarian ikon depicts George, patron saint of soldiers (page 88), killing the dragon that terrorized the people of Silene.

MARKET-GARDENERS
✤
PHOCAS
(?fourth century)

All that is known of Phocas is that he existed and was martyred, probably during the Diocletian persecution of Christians. Tradition has it that he was a market-gardener near Sinope on the southern shores of the Black Sea, who ran an inn for pilgrims and travelers. He used his surplus crops to feed his guests and gave the rest to the poor—hence his patronage of farmers and market-gardeners. One day soldiers arrived at his inn. Unaware of his identity, they told him they had orders to kill a Christian called Phocas and asked him where this man lived. Phocas invited them to stay overnight, promising to give them directions the next morning and, while the soldiers slept, he dug a grave. He revealed himself to his executioners when they awoke and the soldiers, regretfully, carried out their orders. They buried Phocas in the grave he had prepared for himself.

✤

?Fourth century
FEAST DAY: 23 July
CULT: Widely venerated in East
OTHER PATRONAGE: Sailors

✤

BUILDERS

✤
VINCENT FERRER
(1350–1419)

The son of an Englishman living in Spain and a Spanish woman, Vincent was born in Valencia and in 1367 became a Dominican friar. His successes as a preacher to Christians and Jews were spectacular, and in 1378 he was called to Avignon by the schismatic pope Pedro de Luna (Benedict XIII), whose counselor he became. In 1399 he began a preaching tour in France, Spain and Italy; his charismatic, revivalist preachings drew enormous crowds, groups of disciples followed him on his travels, and miracles and mass conversions were recorded in many places.

In 1416 Vincent was instrumental in the ending of the Great Schism of the Church—a measure of his influence: his role in reconstructing Christendom was later to lead to his patronage of builders. Having failed to persuade Benedict XIII to abdicate, he withdrew his support from him, as did Ferdinand of Aragon; Benedict's followers deserted him and Martin V, elected in 1418, was widely recognized. The next year Vincent died while on a preaching tour in Brittany. He was canonized within four decades of his death.

✤

1350 born Valencia, Spain; 1367 became a
Dominican friar; 1378 counselor of Benedict XIII;
1399 began mission in France, Spain, Italy; 1419
died Vannes, Brittany; 1458 canonized
FEAST DAY: 5 April (often celebrated on 6 April)
EMBLEMS: Cardinal's hat; pulpit; trumpet

✤

Vincent Ferrer was a spell-binding preacher.

ECOLOGISTS
✛
FRANCIS OF ASSISI
(1181–1226)

One of the best known and loved of all the saints, Francis was the son of a wealthy cloth merchant in Assisi, Umbria. As a young man he was pleasure-loving and frivolous. When he was 20 war broke out with neighboring Perugia and Francis was taken prisoner. After his release he returned to his old way of life but it gradually held less and less attraction for him. Increasingly, he was concerned for the sick and poor.

When Francis was 25 he heard a voice, in the semi-derelict Church of San Damiano, in Assisi, that told him "Repair my falling house." He took the words literally and sold a bale of his father's cloth to pay for building materials. The conflict between father and son that followed resulted in Francis renouncing his inheritance. He put on the dress of a laborer and went away to "wed Lady Poverty."

Two years later he founded the Friars Minor—the Franciscans—with headquarters near Assisi, and in 1210 Pope Innocent III authorized him and 11 companions to be roving preachers. The order was characterized by its joyful and loving worship of God and its vows of poverty.

By 1219 the Franciscan Order numbered 5,000 friars and was rapidly spreading throughout western Europe. In 1221 Francis produced a new version of his Rule which emphasized poverty and humility, and this was approved by Pope Honorius III in 1223.

Francis of Assisi preaches his famous sermon to the birds.

——————— ✛ ———————

For the last five years of his life Francis held no official position in his order but exemplified his Rule. Some of the best-known incidents about him belong to these years: the inauguration of the Christmas crib in 1223; his sermon to the birds; and above all, his receiving the stigmata. These five wounds of Christ never left him. His last two years were a time of pain, weakness and finally, blindness. He died welcoming "Lady Death," and was canonized two years later.

A man of exceptional spiritual insight, Francis identified with Christ's suffering; and his words and deeds were tangible expressions of his love for God and all creation—the basis for his patronage of ecologists.

——————— ✛ ———————

1181 born Assisi, Umbria; 1201 imprisoned by Perugians; 1207 heard voice in San Damiano Church; 1209 founded Franciscan Order; 1223 approval of new Rule by Pope Honorius III; 1224 experienced stigmata; 1226 died Portiuncula near Assisi; 1228 canonized
FEAST DAY: 4 October
CULT: Early and widespread
OTHER PATRONAGES: Italy; Assisi; animals; animal welfare societies
EMBLEMS: Birds; deer; stigmata

——————— ✛ ———————

LEFT *Francis receives the stigmata—five wounds that resemble the scars on the hands, feet and side of the crucified Christ—that were never to leave him. Giotto, the Florentine artist who painted this and other scenes from the saint's life, was born fewer than 50 years after Francis died.*

ABOVE *Francis's love for creation has made him a popular saint, expecially in the ecology-conscious twentieth century. Medieval writers record that he tamed wild animals and birds—and that they often obeyed his commands.*

RIGHT *A rapt Francis, surrounded by doves, listening to a heavenly melody. The real saint composed a famous hymn to "Brother Sun" shortly before his death, when he was almost blind and in extreme pain from the stigmata.*

SHEPHERDS

✛

BERNADETTE

(1844–1879)

Bernadette was born at Lourdes, in France, the oldest of six children. François Soubirous, her father, was an impoverished miller and she was an ailing and undersized child who suffered from asthma—and was considered slow and backward by many people. Bernadette was a shepherdess, the reason for her patronage of shepherds, and tended her flock on the banks of the River Gave. In 1858, when she was 14 years old, she experienced 18 visions of the Virgin Mary between 11 February and 16 July. The virgin appeared to her in a nearby grotto as a young and beautiful woman and described herself as "the Immaculate Conception." She invoked prayers and penitence, ordered a church to be built and showed Bernadette a forgotten spring—the site of the shrine that today attracts pilgrims from all over the world.

✛

A photograph of Bernadette captures the simple dignity that was one of her outstanding characteristics.

✛

Bernadette's courage and the strength of her belief in her visions were unshaken by searching interrogations by officials of church and state.

Although she suffered acutely from the publicity that followed her experiences, she never lost her patience and dignity. In 1866 she joined a convent in Nevers where she described her role in life as "being ill." She died there in 1879 at the age of 35.

She was canonized in 1933, not because of the many visions she had seen, but for the faith and humility that had characterized her life.

✛

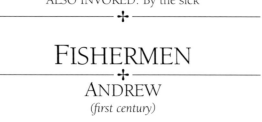

1844 born Lourdes, France; 1858 18 visions of the Virgin Mary; 1866 joined sisters of Notre-Dame of Nevers; 1879 died Nevers; 1933 canonized
FEAST DAY: 16 April (often 18 February in France)
CULT: Centered on basilica at Lourdes; greatest pilgrimage movement of modern Europe
ALSO INVOKED: By the sick

✛

FISHERMEN

✛

ANDREW

(first century)

A fisherman of Bethsaida in Galilee, Andrew was a follower of John the Baptist and the first of Jesus' disciples. Once he had resolved to follow Jesus he fetched his brother Simon (later called Peter) and Jesus called on them both to leave their nets: "Follow me, and I will make you fishers of men." Andrew is always among the first four apostles in the Gospel lists and is mentioned in particular at the miracle of the feeding of the 5,000, where he draws Jesus' attention to the boy carrying the loaves and fishes.

Reports of his life after the Crucifixion are unreliable. He is said to have been a missionary in Asia Minor, Macedonia and south Russia; and to have been martyred, by being bound to an X-shaped cross, in Patras in Greece. Yet another legend describes a journey to Ethiopia. His patronage of fishermen is based on his way of life.

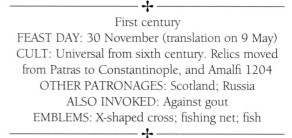

First century
FEAST DAY: 30 November (translation on 9 May)
CULT: Universal from sixth century. Relics moved from Patras to Constantinople, and Amalfi 1204
OTHER PATRONAGES: Scotland; Russia
ALSO INVOKED: Against gout
EMBLEMS: X-shaped cross; fishing net; fish

Andrew's martyrdom; the X-shaped cross on which he died is one of his emblems.

HUNTERS
✛
EUSTACE
(probably apocryphal)

It is unlikely that Eustace existed. Nevertheless he has been venerated as a martyr for centuries and is one of the most popular of saints. According to legend he was a second-century Roman general named Placidas. While hunting near Tivoli he saw a vision of a stag with a luminous crucifix between its antlers and was immediately converted to Christianity—hence his patronage of hunters. He changed his name to Eustace, and was baptized with his wife and sons.

Soon after his conversion Eustace lost his fortune. His wife was abducted by pirates and his two sons disappeared. He retired to a village where he remained for 15 years until the emperor Trajan reinstated him; his wife then returned from captivity and his children were found in a forest. Eustace led his troops on a successful campaign—but was martyred under Hadrian when he refused to give thanks to the Roman gods for his victory. With his wife and two sons he was roasted to death.

✛

Probably apocryphal; said to have died in 118
FEAST DAY: 20 September in West (suppressed in 1969); 2 November in East
ALSO INVOKED: By people in difficult situations

✛

ARCHERS
✛
SEBASTIAN
(died c. 300)

All that is known of Sebastian is that he was an early Christian martyr who was buried on the Appian Way in Rome. Legend depicts him as a native of Gaul (now France), a Christian, who joined the Roman army in c. 283 and rose to become an officer of the imperial guard under the emperor Diocletian. His exhortations strengthened the resolve of two Christian martyrs, Mark and Marcellian, who were awaiting execution in prison—but resulted in his own martyrdom when the emperor discovered that he was a Christian. Sebastian was tied to a tree while archers used his body as a target—the basis of his patronage. They left him for dead, but his wounds were healed by the widow of another saint, Castulus. He then confronted Diocletian for his cruelty to Christians. The emperor was at first speechless but then ordered Sebastian to be clubbed to death. His body was thrown into a sewer.

✛

c. 300 died Rome
FEAST DAY: 20 January
CULT: Widespread in West
OTHER PATRONAGES: Athletes; soldiers
ALSO INVOKED: Against the plague
EMBLEMS: Arrows; crown

✛

LEFT According to legend, Eustace was a Roman soldier called Placidas before he converted to Christianity. His vision of a stag with a crucifix between its antlers was widely represented in scenes of his life. This illustration is from a fifteenth-century Book of Hours.

RIGHT Although early artists portrayed Sebastian as elderly, the saint has more often been depicted as a young man, as in this fifteenth-century painting by Antonio Pollaiulo. Sebastian survived the arrows with which he was pierced, only to be clubbed to death.

SOLDIERS

✢

GEORGE

(died c. 303)

George was a soldier-saint, venerated in the East soon after he was beheaded in Palestine for his faith. Despite his widespread popularity as the personification of Christian chivalry, his martyrdom is the only event in his life that can be accepted as historical fact. Of the many legends that surround him, the best known is his battle with a dragon while on his way to the Holy Land.

According to this tradition, the citizens of Silene in Libya were terrorized by a dragon that lived in a nearby lake or marsh, poisoning the air of the city with its breath. To appease the monster, the Silenians offered it first two sheep a day and later two children who were chosen by lot. Eventually Princess Cleolinda, the king's daughter, was selected. As she walked towards the dragon, dressed as a bride, she met George who promised to save her through the power of Jesus Christ. He pierced the dragon with a lance and, using Cleolinda's girdle as a leash, led it back to the city as

though it was a tame dog—and then killed it. In gratitude for Silene's deliverance 15,000 men were baptized that same day. George gave his reward to the Church, the priests and the poor, then continued on his travels.

Although he was known in England and Ireland in the eighth and ninth centuries, his popularity and patronage of soldiers became firmly established in the eleventh century, when returning crusaders described how he had appeared to the Christian army in a vision before the Saracens' defeat in 1098. He was adopted as patron saint of England in the fourteenth century.

✢

c. 303 died, probably at Diospolis (now Lydda) in Palestine
FEAST DAY: 23 April
CULT: Widespread in East; reached peak in West in thirteenth and fourteenth centuries. Reduced to local status in 1969
OTHER PATRONAGES: Armorers; butchers; saddlers; boy scouts; Venice; Germany; Genoa; Portugal; Catalonia; Greece; England
ALSO INVOKED: Against skin diseases
EMBLEMS: Armor; dragon

✢

✢

In a famous legend George saved the Princess Cleolinda from a dragon by wounding the monster with his lance; he then tamed it by using her girdle as a lead. In early Christian tradition a dragon was a symbol of evil.

✢

Through the centuries sailors have believed that St Elmo's fire—the electrical discharge that sometimes illuminates ships' masts during stormy weather—is a sign that the saint will protect them from the elements.

SAILORS
ELMO
(died c. 300)

Elmo is known to have been a bishop of Formiae in the Campagna, Italy, who was martyred under the emperor Diocletian. According to one legend, he was a Syrian bishop who fled persecution to become a hermit on Mount Lebanon. Here he was captured and martyred by having his intestines drawn out by a windlass. Because of the instrument's similarity to a capstan, sailors invoke him as their patron saint. Another legend relates how on one occasion Elmo preached fearlessly through a violent storm undeterred by a thunderbolt. The bluish electrical discharge that can be seen flickering round a masthead before and after a storm, called St. Elmo's fire, is a sign that the ship is under the saint's protection.

c. 300 died Formiae, Italy
FEAST DAY: 2 June
ALSO KNOWN AS: Erasmus
CULT: Throughout Europe in Middle Ages.
ALSO INVOKED: By navigators; women in labor.
Against appendicitis; intestinal troubles
EMBLEM: Windlass

ASTRONAUTS AND PILOTS
JOSEPH OF COPERTINO
(1603–1663)

An ecstatic and mystic who was nicknamed "the flying friar" because of the frequency with which he levitated, Joseph's early years were spent in poverty in Copertino near Brindisi, Italy. His parents were so poor that his father, who died shortly after his birth, had to sell the family home to pay his debts and Joseph himself was born in a garden shed.

His mother resented "the gaper," as her sickly, slow witted son was known, and Joseph, who was passionate about the correct performance of his religious duties, attempted to join the Franciscan Conventuals and the Capuchins. Initially his clumsiness and forgetfulness made him unacceptable to both, but his mother eventually found him a position as a stable boy at a Franciscan house at La Grottella. Here Joseph improved to such an extent that, at the age of 22, he was admitted as a novice. He was ordained in 1628.

From then on he led a life of extreme austerity, characterized by healings, ecstasies during which he was impervious to any external stimulus and, in particular, by repeated occasions when his body was

Joseph of Copertino was famous for his levitations; on one occasion he flew through a church, from door to door, over the heads of the congregation.

✦

raised and moved through the air, apparently by a supernatural force. No less than 70 of these levitations—the reason for his patronage of pilots and astronauts—were recorded during his 17 years at La Grottella.

Although unimpeachable witnesses attested to these extraordinary phenomena, Joseph's superiors were disturbed by his raptures. They banned him from celebrating mass publicly and from taking part in the daily life of his community. In the late 1630s they sent him to Pope Urban VIII, at the sight of whom he fell

into a state of ecstasy. Joseph remained an embarrassment to the authorities for the rest of his life, during the last ten years of which he was moved from one friary to another and kept in strict seclusion. He died at Osimo in 1663.

The people venerated him as much as the Church was disturbed by him, and he was canonized just over a hundred years after his death—not for the supernatural phenomena that had distinguished his life but for the extreme patience and humility with which he had borne its trials.

✦

1603 born Copertino, Italy; 1625 admitted to
La Grottella friary as novice;
1628 ordained; c. 1639 visit to Pope Urban VIII;
1639–54 friaries at Assisi (13 years),
Pietrorossa, Fossombrone;
1655 Assisi; 1657 friary at Osimo;
1663 died Osimo;
1757 canonized
FEAST DAY: 18 September
CULT: Confined to local calendars since 1969

✦

MOUNTAINEERS
✦
BERNARD OF MONTJOUX
(c. 996–c. 1081)

Bernard's patronage of mountaineers is a natural extension of his life's work. For 42 years, as vicar-general of the Alpine diocese of Aosta in Italy, he visited every valley and mountain in his jurisdiction ministering to the region's scattered inhabitants. He also had particular responsibility for the travelers—often French and German pilgrims on their way to Rome—who crossed the Alps by the two passes that led to Aosta. The dangers they faced were great: some people froze to death, some lost their way, some blundered into snowdrifts. Those who survived were at risk from robbers.

Bernard cleared the robbers from the passes—now called the Little and Great St. Bernard—and established hospices to receive all travelers regardless of their nationality and religion, at the summit of each

Saint Bernard dogs, named after the saint, were first bred as guard and guide dogs. Later they developed a talent for rescuing lost travelers.

✟

pass. He died at the age of about 85, on a journey to Novara in Lombardy and in 1923 Pius XI, himself an alpinist, named him patron saint of mountaineers.

The hospices were run by Augustinian canons, the order that is still responsible for them today. The dogs named after St. Bernard were first bred and trained by the canons in the seventeenth century.

✟

c. 996 born; c. 1081 died Novara
FEAST DAY: 28 May
ALSO KNOWN AS: Bernard of Menthon; of Aosta
OTHER PATRONAGE: Travelers in the Alps
EMBLEMS: White dog; angel holding crozier

✟

PILGRIMS

✟

FAITH
(?third century)

Faith may have been a virgin martyr who died at Agen in Gascony, France; but her legend, which makes her a young girl who was roasted to death on a brazen bed and then beheaded, is fictitious. She is also confused with one of the three mythical sisters, Faith, Hope and Charity. Her cult, which was centered on her relics at Conques, in France, spread with remarkable rapidity along the pilgrim routes to and from Compostela—hence her patronage of pilgrims. Her many legends portray her as a capricious patron: in return for offering her protection she expected substantial donations to her church at Conques and could turn against the ungenerous.

✟

?Third century
FEAST DAY: 6 October
ALSO KNOWN AS: Foi; Foy
CULT: Widespread in England, Italy, Spain, South America
OTHER PATRONAGES: Soldiers; prisoners
EMBLEMS: Gridiron; sword; rods

✟

Faith's reliquary, studded with pilgrims' gifts of precious stones, is in the abbey at Conques.

MISSIONARIES
✢
THERESA OF LISIEUX
(1873–1897)

✢

*Veneration for
Theresa of Lisieux
began immediately
after the
publication of her
autobiography.*

✢

Also known as the "Little Flower of Jesus," Theresa was one of four sisters who became Carmelite nuns in the same convent. She was born in Alençon, Normandy, and when she was four years old her father, Louis Martin, moved the family to Lisieux after her mother's death.

Theresa was educated by Benedictine nuns, and was only 14 when she experienced her conversion and determined to become a Carmelite. She entered the order at the unusually early age of 15.

This postcard was published soon after Theresa of Lisieux's canonization in 1925.

She performed all the duties demanded of her by the austere Carmelite rule with extraordinary dedication and became assistant to the novice mistress when she was 22. She considered volunteering for missionary work in Hanoi (now in Vietnam)—the basis for her patronage of missionaries—but contracted tuberculosis and died after 18 months of heroic suffering.

In her autobiography, *The Story of a Soul*, written on the orders of her prioress and edited by her eldest sister Marie, Theresa wrote that she would "let fall a shower of roses"—miracles and favors—after her death. The book, which was published soon after she died, was an immediate and sensational success and, although Theresa had previously been unknown, veneration for her became widespread. Innumerable miracles were attributed to her and she was canonized in 1925, less than 30 years after her death.

✢

1873 born Alençon, Normandy; 1877 Lisieux,
Normandy; 1888 entered Carmelite order; 1895
appointed assistant to novice mistress;
1897 died Lisieux; 1925 canonized
FEAST DAY: 1 October
CULT: Immediate; centered on basilica at Lisieux
(dedicated in 1954)
OTHER PATRONAGES: France; florists;
flower growers
EMBLEM: Bunch of roses

✢

Theresa of Lisieux is traditionally portrayed holding a bunch of roses, an allusion to the 'shower of roses'— miracles and other favors—that she wrote about in her autobiography.

CHAPTER SIX

---✛---

PERSONAL FEARS AND PROBLEMS

... for I am desolate and afflicted.
PSALMS 25:16

---✛---

MATRIMONIAL PROBLEMS

✛

RITA
(1377–1447)

Rita's overwhelming desire as a child was to be a nun. But her elderly parents were determined that she should marry and Rita, who was submissive to authority throughout her life, deferred to their wishes. Her husband was ill-mannered, unfaithful and his rages terrified even his neighbors. Nevertheless, she lived with him uncomplainingly for 18 years—the reason why she is invoked by people with matrimonial problems—until he was killed in a vendetta.

To Rita's distress, her two sons, who had inherited much of their father's character, swore to avenge his death. She prayed that they should die rather than commit the terrible crime of murder—a prayer that was answered when they became fatally ill. She tended them as they lay dying and, as a result, both young men were filled with forgiveness.

Rita finally achieved her ambition when in 1407 she

---✛---

LEFT Patrick is invoked against snakes (page 104) and is often portrayed driving them before him.

Rita appears to be wounded by a crown of thorns.

---✛---

entered the Augustinian convent at Cascia in Umbria. Through prayer and self-mortification, she became a mystic, and devoted herself to converting sinners and caring for sick nuns. For the last 15 years of her life she suffered the pain of a chronic wound that appeared on her head as though she had been wearing a crown of thorns. She died of tuberculosis in 1447.

1377 born Roccaporena, Umbria;
1407 entered Augustinian convent, Cascia,
Umbria; 1447 died Cascia;
1900 canonized
FEAST DAY: 22 May
CULT: Widespread; especially popular in Italy,
France, Spain, Eire, the United States,
the Philippines
OTHER PATRONAGES: Desperate causes;
parenthood
ALSO INVOKED: Against infertility

HOMELESSNESS

BENEDICT JOSEPH LABRE
(1748–1783)

Benedict Joseph Labre was a pilgrim and holy wandering man, not initially through choice—in his late teens he tried unsuccessfully to join the Cistercian and then the Carthusian order—but because he came to accept that he was too unstable for the monastic way of life. The oldest of the 15 children of a Boulogne shopkeeper, he left his prosperous home when he was 22 to go on pilgrimage to Rome. For four years he traveled on foot through France, Italy, Switzerland and Spain, visiting the holy shrines. His clothes were verminous rags and he slept, more often than not, in the open. He accepted gifts of food but money was given away, or shared.

When he reached Rome, in 1774, he spent his days praying in churches and his nights sleeping in the ruins of the Colosseum until his failing health forced him to seek shelter in a hospice for the destitute. He collapsed on the steps of Santa Maria dei Monti on Easter Saturday in 1783, and died in the back room of a butcher's shop.

He was canonized just over 100 years later, in 1881. Because of his way of life he is the patron saint of the homeless and tramps.

1748 born Amette near Boulogne, France; 1766–70
attempted to join Cistercians and Carthusians;
1770–74 pilgrimage through Europe; 1774–83 lived
in Rome; 1783 died; 1881 canonized
FEAST DAY: 16 April

In this painting by Canaletto the Colosseum looks much as it did when Benedict Joseph Labre slept there. He lived in Rome for about nine years and was acclaimed a saint immediately after his death.

IMPOVERISHMENT

✝

MARTIN OF TOURS

(316–397)

The son of a pagan Roman officer, Martin was born in Upper Pannonia (now Hungary) and educated in Pavia in northern Italy. He knew from the age of ten that he intended to become a Christian but was enrolled in the Imperial cavalry five years later, against his will and before he had been baptized. At Amiens one bitterly cold night he gave half of his cloak to a freezing and naked beggar—and soon afterwards saw a vision in which Christ appeared wearing it. As a result of this event—the basis of his invocation against impoverishment—Martin was finally baptized.

He asked for a discharge from the army, believing that as a Christian he was not allowed to fight, and was accused of cowardice. His answer, according to legend, was to stand unarmed in the battle line, holding only a cross—at the sight of which the enemy surrendered. Martin was given his discharge and, in his early 20s, left the army to become a disciple of St. Hilary of Poitiers. He later traveled in Italy and Dalmatia. He lived as a hermit for ten years before rejoining Hilary, who encouraged him to found a community of monk-hermits at Ligugé—the first monastery in Gaul (now France). In 372 Martin, then 56, accepted the episcopate of Tours. Although he was reluctant to take on the appointment and continued to live as a monk—first in a cell near his church and later at Marmoutier where he established

Martin of Tours was a soldier in the Roman army when he gave part of his cloak to a beggar.

✝

another great monastic center—he was zealous in discharging his duties. He was also a dedicated missionary, who traveled in the remotest parts of his diocese by foot, by donkey and by boat; and a wonder-worker whose miracles included healing lepers and raising a man from the dead.

Martin opposed Arianism and Priscillianism, the two great heresies of the day, but condemned the practice of putting heretics to death: he interceded with the emperor Maximus in an unsuccessful attempt to prevent the execution of Priscillian and others for heresy, arguing that it was sufficient to declare them heretics and excommunicate them.

The first great pioneer of Western monasticism, Martin died in Candes; more than 2,000 monks accompanied his body on its return to Tours.

✝

316 born Upper Pannonia (Hungary); 331 enrolled in Roman army; 339 left army; joined St. Hilary of Poitiers; 372 appointed bishop of Tours; 397 died Candes, near Tours
FEAST DAY: 11 November
CULT: Immediate and widespread
OTHER PATRONAGES: Soldiers; horses; riders; geese; wine-growers
EMBLEMS: Globe of fire; goose

✝

The occasion when Martin of Tours divided his cloak
with his sword and gave one half to a cold and starving
beggar has been depicted by numerous artists
and craftsmen, and immortalized
in stained glass (above) and oils (left).

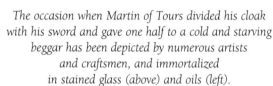

LEFT Martin of Tours is
wearing the stirrups of a
cavalry officer in this
illustration from a
fourteenth-century
manuscript. As bishop of
Tours he evangelized the
rural regions of Gaul and
was a pioneer of Western
monasticism. His biography,
written by his friend and
associate Sulpicius Severus,
was extremely popular in
the Middle Ages and his cult
was widespread. In France,
over 4,000 churches are
dedicated to him.

*A fifteenth-century Hungarian
painting of Martin of Tours. The
saint has given his name to the spell
of fine weather that can occur
around 11 November, his feast day.
Known as St. Martin's Summer, it
is the English counterpart of the
American Indian summer.*

MISFORTUNE
✛
AGRICOLA OF AVIGNON
(c. 630–700)

According to tradition, Agricola was the son of a saint—Magnus, bishop of Avignon. When he was 16 he became a monk at Lérins, and remained there for the next 14 years until his father summoned him to Avignon where, at the age of about 30, he was appointed bishop.

In Avignon he built a church served by the monks of Lérins, and a convent for Benedictine nuns. Agricola is renowned for ending an invasion of storks by his blessing. He is invoked against misfortune as the special protector of Avignon, whose patron saint he became in 1647.

✛

c. 630 born; c. 632 appointed bishop
of Avignon; 700 died
FEAST DAY: 2 September
OTHER PATRONAGE: Avignon
ALSO INVOKED: Against plague. For
good weather; rain
EMBLEM: Stork

✛

Avignon bridge; Agricola was the city's bishop.

LOSING KEYS
✛
ZITA
(1218–1272)

Zita was born into a devoutly Christian family: her parents were devoted to their faith, her elder sister was a nun and her uncle was a hermit whom many local people regarded as a saint. She herself became a servant at the age of 12 in the household of Pagano di Fatinelli, a wealthy weaver from Lucca in Italy, and remained with the family until her death 48 years later.

Her fellow-workers initially resented her because of the punctiliousness with which she performed her duties; and she infuriated her master with her lavish generosity to the poor: she frequently gave her own food to them, and often gave her bed to a beggar and spent the night sleeping on the ground.

Eventually, however, her goodness and patience won the confidence of servants and employer alike. During her later years, Zita was freed from much of her domestic work so that she could devote herself to caring for the sick and poor and ministering to prisoners who had been sentenced to death.

Miracles were attributed to her during her life—on one occasion angels miraculously baked bread on her behalf while she was praying—and on her death she was declared a saint by the acclaim of the people of Lucca; she was not, however, formally canonized for more than four centuries.

Because her work was part of her religion she is the patron of maidservants and invoked by housewives and servants, especially when they lose their keys.

✛

1218 born Montsagrati near Lucca, Italy;
1231 entered service of Pagano di Fatinelli, Lucca;
1272 died Lucca; 1696 canonized
FEAST DAY: 27 April
ALSO KNOWN AS: Sitha; Citha
CULT: Immediate; centered on her tomb in Lucca.
Widespread from late Middle Ages
OTHER PATRONAGE: Maidservants
EMBLEMS: Bag; keys; loaves; rosary

✛

LOST PROPERTY
✛
ANTONY OF PADUA
(1195–1231)

Antony was a teacher and preacher so charismatic that the crowds who came to hear him during the nine years of his mission could not be contained in the churches. Instead, they gathered in the market-places to hear his attacks on usury and avarice, the two great enemies of the poor.

A Portuguese nobleman by birth, Antony joined the Augustinian canons at an early age but when he was 25 moved to the Franciscan friars, who sent him to work among the Muslims of Morocco. But ill-health forced him to return within the year to Assisi, where his exceptional talents for preaching and teaching were soon discovered. He was chosen by St. Francis of Assisi to teach theology to the friars at Padua and Bologna, and later preached against the Albigensian heretics in southern France. From 1227 to 1230 he ruled the Franciscan province in northern Italy and was commissioned by Pope Gregory IX to produce a series of sermons for feast days. He died young, at 36, and was canonized a year after his death, in 1232.

He gained a major reputation as a worker of wonders and miracles. One of the best-known stories about him—the reason he is invoked to find lost property—is that a novice borrowed his psalter without his permission, and was compelled to return it by a terrifying apparition.

✛

1195 born Lisbon, Portugal; 1220 joined
Franciscans, sailed for Africa; 1221 returned
to Assisi; 1230 retired to Padua; 1231 died;
1232 canonized; 1263 relics translated at Padua;
1946 declared a Doctor of the Church
FEAST DAY: 13 June
CULT: Widespread; strong in France, Brazil,
Portugal, Ireland, USA
OTHER PATRONAGES: Portugal; Brazil
ALSO INVOKED: By barren and pregnant women;
the poor; travelers. Against shipwreck
EMBLEMS: Christ child; book; lily

✛

✛

Antony of Padua holds the infant Christ in his arms—a portrayal of a vision in which the Virgin Mary and Jesus appeared to the saint. The Christ Child is one of his emblems; two others—a lily for purity, and a book—are also shown in this engraving.

✛

IMPRISONMENT

✠

LEONARD OF NOBLAC
(?sixth century)

Although there is no trace of Leonard before the eleventh century, he is one of the most popular medieval saints. According to legend, he was a Frankish noble. King Clovis I was his godfather and offered him a bishopric—which he refused. Instead he retired to the Abbey of Micy near Orléans and later became a hermit in the nearby forest of Noblac.

Clovis was hunting in the forest one day, accompanied by his wife, when she went into dangerous and difficult labor. Leonard's prayers saved both mother and child and Clovis gave him as much land as he could ride round in one night on a donkey. Leonard used this endowment to found the Abbey of Noblac.

Leonard's invocation against imprisonment is sometimes linked with the similarity of his name to *lien*, the French word for fetter. It was given an impetus when in 1103 Bohemond, prince of Antioch, released from captivity in the Holy Land, went to Noblac and gave thanks to the saint for his deliverance.

✠

?Sixth century
FEAST DAY: 6 November
CULT: Widespread in West in Middle Ages
OTHER PATRONAGE: Childbirth
ALSO INVOKED: Against robbers
EMBLEMS: Chain; fetters; manacles

✠

PRISONERS UNDER SENTENCE OF DEATH

✠

DISMAS
(died c. 30)

Dismas is the name traditionally given to one of the two criminals who were crucified with Jesus. Also known as "the Good Thief," he rebuked his companion who challenged Jesus, as Christ, to save himself. The good thief was rewarded when Jesus told him: "today you shall be with me in paradise"—hence his patronage of prisoners, particularly those under sentence of death.

This episode, recorded in Luke's Gospel, is all that is known of him. The legend that he was one of the leaders of a band of brigands who waylaid the Holy Family, when they were fleeing to Egypt after Jesus' birth, came much later and is improbable. Dismas' name derives from the Greek word *dysme* (dying).

✠

c. 30 died Jerusalem
FEAST DAY: 25 March
OTHER PATRONAGES: Thieves; undertakers
EMBLEM: Tall cross

✠

SLAVERY

✠

PETER CLAVER
(1580–1654)

Born in Catalonia, in Spain and educated at the University of Barcelona, Peter became a Jesuit when he was 20. At the college of Palma, in Majorca, he discovered a vocation to be a missionary and, having studied theology at Barcelona, embarked for the New World in 1610.

He was ordained a priest in 1615 and from 1616 worked with Alfonso de Sandoval, the great Jesuit missionary, ministering to the slaves of Cartagena, now in Colombia.

For the next 33 years Peter cared for and preached to more than 300,000 black slaves. Brought from their African homelands in the most horrible conditions, suffering from cruelty and deprivation, often without any water or nourishment and decimated by disease, those who survived were destined for the mines and plantations of South America.

Peter and his followers gave them medicine, food and drink when they arrived in Cartagena, taught them the elements of the Christian faith and sought to restore their human dignity—the basis for his patronage of slaves.

The monastery of St. Peter Claver at Cartagena, Colombia. Peter Claver baptized more than 3,000,000 slaves during his years as a missionary, and is said to have heard over 5,000 confessions in one year alone. He also cared for lepers and sufferers from "St Anthony's Fire," a painful skin disease.

✥

He preached to prisoners and the poor and sick irrespective of race and color, and visited slaves at the mines and plantations, in prison and in hospital.

Although he had some support from the wealthier inhabitants of Cartagena, many plantation owners complained that he wasted their slaves' time and blamed him when they misbehaved. He also alienated the ecclesiastical establishment, partly because of his obstinacy and difficult temperament.

Nevertheless, after his death in 1654—after four years of paralysis and constant pain during which he was neglected by his followers—he was accorded great honor by the Church.

✥

1580 born Verdu, Catalonia, Spain; 1600 became a Jesuit; 1610 went to Cartagena, Colombia; 1615 ordained; 1616 began missionary work with African slaves; 1650 fell ill and retired from mission; 1654 died Cartagena; 1888 canonized
FEAST DAY: 9 September
OTHER PATRONAGE: Missions to native Africans

✥

POLITICAL IMPRISONMENT
✥
MAXIMILIAN KOLBE
(1894–1941)

The son of poor but pious parents, Maximilian was born near Lodz in Poland in 1894. In 1910 he joined the Franciscan order, then studied at Rome and was ordained in 1919 when he was 25. Soon after his ordination he was diagnosed as suffering from tuberculosis and returned to Poland where he taught in a seminary.

From this base he founded a magazine for Christian readers in Cracow; it was a great success and later its headquarters was moved to Niepokalanow, near Warsaw, and run from a newly-founded Franciscan friary. Despite his illness Maximilian established a similar community in Japan.

In 1936 his order recalled him to Niepokalanow and appointed him superior of the friary there three years later. When the Nazis invaded Poland he advised most of the community's 700 brothers to disperse. But he remained and Niepokalanow became a refugee camp, which housed 3,000 Poles and 1,500 Jews. Maximilian continued to publish newspapers that were consistently patriotic and anti-Nazi. As a result he was arrested and taken to Auschwitz concentration camp in May 1941.

For the next three months he continued his work as a priest, hearing confession and officiating at masses. In August he offered himself in the place of a younger man who had been condemned to die by starvation.

He survived in the death cell for 14 days and was finally killed with a lethal injection.

When he was canonized in 1982 the man whose life he had saved was in the congregation. Maximilian stands as an example of great heroism among political prisoners.

1894 born Zdunska Wola near Lodz, Poland;
1910 became a Franciscan; 1919 ordained;
1936 superior of Niepokalanow;
1941 died Auschwitz; 1982 canonized
FEAST DAY: 14 August

A terminus at Auschwitz, where Maximilian Kolbe died.

FEAR OF SNAKES

PATRICK

(c. 390–c. 461)

The great evangelizer of the Irish was born in the west of Britain and was Romano-British in origin. Patrick was comparatively irreligious when, at the age of 16, he was captured by pirates. He was a slave in Ireland, working as a herdsman, for the next six years during which he learned to pray and take religion seriously. Eventually he escaped and returned home a changed man. He trained for the priesthood and in c. 432 returned to Ireland as a missionary.

There was already a bishop, Palladius, and a small community of Christians, but they had made little

Patrick expels snakes from Ireland.

---

impression on the Irish. Patrick and his followers diffused Christianity widely in the north of Ireland, encouraged the spread of monasticism and built up a network of territorial sees. In 444 he set up his episcopal see at Armagh, from where he organized numerous missions to Ireland's pagan inhabitants. His writings, including the *Confessio* and the *Letter to Coroticus*, reveal him as man of determination and humility with a deep trust in God, rather than a learned scholar.

After his death many legends grew up around Patrick. One was that he explained the Trinity by reference to the shamrock, another that he expelled all snakes from Ireland. As a result his emblems are shamrocks and snakes and he is invoked by people who are frightened of snakes.

---

c. 390 born western Britain; c. 406 captured by pirates; c. 413 returned to Britain; c. 432 returned to Ireland; c. 461 died Saul, County Down, Ireland

FEAST DAY: 17 March
CULT: Spread from Ireland to Europe; popular in Europe in Middle Ages; more recently in North America and Australia
OTHER PATRONAGE: Ireland
EMBLEMS: Snake; shamrock

FEAR OF INSECTS

GRATUS OF AOSTA
(died c. 470)

A ll that is known of the historical Gratus, the patron saint of Aosta, is that he signed the acts of the synod of Milan, in 451, as a priest; and that as bishop of Aosta he was present at the translation of various saints in the city in c. 470, and died soon afterwards. A canon of Aosta cathedral composed a fictitious tale about him in 1285, in which he traveled to the Holy Land and returned with the head of John the Baptist.

After his death, Gratus was noted as a worker of miracles; a particular speciality was his power, when invoked, to drive away plagues of insects, as in 1450 in the Tarentaise region, in France. For this reason he is called upon for protection by those who fear insects.

---

c. 470 died
FEAST DAY: 7 September
CULT: Very popular in the Aosta area

FEAR OF WASPS

FRIARD
(c. 511–577)

T he son of a poor laborer, Friard was born at Besné near Nantes, in France. Although uneducated, he was a religious man and a contemplative whose ways were mocked by the local peasants. All this changed when at harvest time a great swarm of wasps emerged from the ground and stung his tormentors, who

challenged Friard to rid them of the menace; he duly did so through prayer. This is the basis of his invocation by those who fear wasps. Friard subsequently retired with two companions to an island in the River Loire, to live as a hermit; he died in 577.

---

c. 511 born Besné, France; hermit on island in the River Loire; 577 died; buried Besné
FEAST DAY: 1 August

FEAR OF RATS AND MICE

GERTRUDE OF NIVELLES
(626–659)

G ertrude was brought up in a religious household: her father, Pépin of Landen (Charlemagne's ancestor) and her mother, Itta, were dedicated Christians, and her sister Begga is also a saint. After Pépin's death in 640, when Gertrude was 14, his widow founded a monastery for monks and nuns at Nivelles, now in Belgium. She became one of its nuns and her young daughter was its first abbess. Gertrude was renowned for her hospitality to pilgrims and the abbey became a center for missionary work, particularly by Irish monks.

Gertrude's ascetic lifestyle exhausted her and at the age of 30 she resigned her office to her niece. She died soon afterwards. She is invoked against rats and mice, probably as a survival of a local pagan myth.

---

626 born Landen, Belgium; c. 645 became first abbess of Nivelles; c. 655 resigned as abbess; 659 died Nivelles
FEAST DAY: 17 March
CULT: Widespread in the Low Countries; spread to England
OTHER PATRONAGES: Travelers; pilgrims
ALSO INVOKED: On behalf of the recently dead
EMBLEMS: Rats; mice

CHAPTER SEVEN

✛

DISEASES AND ILL HEALTH

... sick of the palsy, grievously tormented.
MATTHEW 8:6

————————— ✛ —————————

EPIDEMICS

————— ✛ —————

ROCH
(c. 1350–c. 1380)

Only two facts about Roch are known with any kind of certainty: that he was born in Montpellier, France, and ministered to plague victims in Italy. Tradition relates that he was the son of a wealthy merchant and that after the death of his parents, when he was 18, he gave away his riches and went on a pilgrimage to Rome, where he stayed for three years.

On his return journey he caught the plague at Piacenza, and was said to have been nursed back to health by a dog. He then cured sufferers from the plague by making the sign of the cross over them—the reason why he is invoked against epidemics.

Descriptions of his later life vary. According to one story, he returned home so emaciated that his uncle had him put in prison as an impostor. Another version relates that he was imprisoned at Angleria in Lombardy as a spy. In both versions he died in prison.

————————— ✛ —————————

RIGHT Roch is depicted in a pilgrim's robes, holding a pilgrim's staff. The dark spot on his leg is an allusion to the plague—its first symptoms usually appeared on the thigh.

LEFT St. Lucy is invoked against blindness (page 114). Here she carries two eyes on a platter.

————————— ✛ —————————

c. 1350 born Montpellier; 1368–71 in Rome;
c. 1380 died Montpellier or Angleria
FEAST DAY: 16 August
ALSO KNOWN AS: Rocco; Rock; Rollox
CULT: Spread rapidly in Italy, France and Germany

————————— ✛ —————————

THE SICK
✛
JOHN OF GOD
(1495–1550)

Most of John's life was spent in secular pursuits—born in Portugal, he was first a mercenary who fought for Spain in Hungary, then a shepherd in Andalusia—and he was 40 before he repented of his former ways of life. Filled with remorse he was determined to help the poor and needy, and only with difficulty was he dissuaded from seeking martyrdom by helping Christian slaves in North Africa. Instead he sold holy books to the people of Gibraltar—and was so successful that within a few years, in 1538, he was able to open a shop in Granada.

Soon after his arrival there, John suffered a period of madness after hearing a sermon of John of Avila, tearing his hair and giving away his books. Counseled by John of Avila, he recovered within the year and in 1539 set up a hospital in the city, where he and his followers tended the poor and sick, vagrants and prostitutes—the reason for his patronage of the sick. He aroused suspicion and hostility, but such was his success that the bishop accepted him as a monk. He died as a result of rescuing a man drowning in a flood.

John had never considered establishing a religious order, but 20 years after his death in 1550, his followers were constituted an order of Hospitallers, and he was named as its founder.

✛

1495 born Montemor-o-Novo, Portugal;
1522 mercenary for the count of Oroprusa, Castile;
1535 converted; 1538 opened shop in Granada;
1539 after period of insanity, founded hospital in Granada; 1550 died; 1570 order of Hospitallers constituted and spread throughout West;
1690 canonized
FEAST DAY: 8 March
OTHER PATRONAGES: Booksellers; printers
EMBLEMS: Alms; crown of thorns; heart

✛

John of God gave his name to an order of Hospitallers.

MENTAL ILLNESS
✛
DYMPHNA
(Existence doubtful)

The legendary Dymphna was the Christian daughter of a pagan Irish or British chieftain who, with her chaplain, fled to Antwerp and then to nearby Gheel to escape the incestuous advances of her father. She was found by her avenging father who put both of them to death.

This legend was prompted by the discovery of the relics of a man and a woman—with an inscription naming one Dymphna—at Gheel in the early thirteenth century. When the bones were translated remarkable cures of the insane and epileptics were recorded, and Dymphna soon became the patron saint of the mentally ill. By the end of the thirteenth century Gheel had a major hospital, which ever since has provided enlightened care for the insane.

Existence doubtful
FEAST DAY: 15 May
ALSO KNOWN AS: Dympna
OTHER PATRONAGE: Sleepwalkers
ALSO INVOKED: Against epilepsy; possession
by the devil

EARACHE
POLYCARP
(c. 69–c. 155)

A close associate of John the Apostle—a man "who had seen the Lord"—Polycarp was in his 30s when he became bishop of Smyrna (now in Turkey), a position he held for the next 50 years. He defended orthodox Christian belief against the Gnostic heresy, but agreed to disagree with the bishop of Rome about how the date of Easter should accurately be calculated.

Polycarp was burned alive with 12 of his disciples.

Obstinate and conservative, he is said to have stated that he would rather stop his ears than hear and argue against heretical doctrines—the reason for his invocation against earache.

Polycarp died for his faith with 12 of his followers during the persecutions of Marcus Aurelius, betrayed and arrested at a farm near Smyrna. Authentic records of his trial and execution describe how, when asked to curse Christ, he replied: "I have been his servant for 86 years and he has done me no wrong. How can I blaspheme my King and Savior?"

Although the crowd called for him to be thrown to the lions, he was, more mercifully, pierced with a sword and then burned.

c. 69 born; c. 96 bishop of Smyrna;
c. 155 died Smyrna
FEAST DAY: 23 February
CULT: Immediate; widespread in East and West

HANGOVERS
BIBIANA
(died c. 361)

B ibiana was a virgin who was martyred in Rome. A colorful but improbable tale of her death records that she was tied to a pillar and scourged until she died. A fellow Christian buried her with her mother and sister, who had also been martyred, and a church was founded on the site. In its garden grew a herb with the power to cure epilepsy and headaches—and also alleviate the effects of over-indulgence, the reason she is invoked against hangovers.

c. 361 died Rome
FEAST DAY: 2 December
ALSO KNOWN AS: Viviana
CULT: Widespread in Italy, Germany and Spain;
confined to Bibiana's basilica in Rome since 1969
ALSO INVOKED: Against epilepsy; headache
EMBLEMS: Branch; pillar

SORE THROATS
✝
IGNATIUS OF ANTIOCH
(died c. 107)

Ignatius was bishop of Antioch from c. 69, but little is known of him until his arrest during the emperor Trajan's persecution of the Christians, and subsequent journey to Rome for public execution. However, he may have been a disciple of St. Peter and St. Paul and of St. John and, according to legend, was the child Jesus set in the midst of his disciples when he told them, "whoso shall receive one such little child in my name receiveth me."

On his journey Ignatius wrote seven letters to his followers which provide invaluable information about the organization and doctrine of the early Church. When he arrived in Rome, he was killed by wild beasts, probably in the Colosseum. He is invoked as healer of sore throats because, even amid all his torments, he never ceased to call out the name of Jesus.

✝

c. 107 died Rome
FEAST DAY: 17 October
ALSO KNOWN AS: Theophoros (God-Bearer)
CULT: Widespread in East and West; relics at Saint Peter's, Rome
EMBLEMS: Lions; chains

✝

✝

Ignatius, bishop of Antioch, was one of the earliest Christian martyrs.

✝

MIGRAINE
✝
GEREON
(died ?304)

Gereon, who may have been a soldier, was martyred at Cologne, allegedly by beheading, probably in the early fourth century. According to later legend he and some companions were lost members of the Theban Legion, a Christian unit in the Roman army, most of whose members were massacred by the emperor Maximian when they refused to sacrifice to the pagan gods. Gereon became a popular saint. He is represented as a Roman soldier or medieval knight in art. He is one of a number of saints who died by decapitation and were invoked against migraine.

✝

?304 died Cologne
FEAST DAY: 10 October
ALSO INVOKED: Against headaches

✝

TOOTHACHE
✝
KEA
(?sixth century)

Although Kea gave his name to places in Devon, Cornwall and Brittany, details of his life are obscure. According to tradition he was a nobleman from Glastonbury, who traveled as a monk and bishop in the south-west of England and then to Brittany founding churches. One legend tells how a wicked prince, Theodoric, was so enraged to see Kea harnessing stags to the plough that he knocked out one of his teeth. The saint went to wash out his mouth at the fountain near his hermitage at Kea. The waters have cured toothache, against which Kea is invoked, ever since.

✝

?Sixth century
FEAST DAY: 5 November
ALSO KNOWN AS: Ke; Kay; Kenan; Quay

✝

HEADACHES

✠

STEPHEN

(died c. 35)

Stephen the Deacon was a Greek-speaking Jew and the first Christian martyr. The circumstances of his conversion are unknown, but his death at Jerusalem is recorded in the Acts of the Apostles. Stephen was distinguished by his strong personality, erudition and eloquence and the apostles entrusted him with the distribution of alms to the faithful. His power as a preacher aroused hostility and he was denounced to the Jewish council, the Sanhedrin, which summoned him to explain himself. He made his case at great

✠

RIGHT Stephen, the first martyr, is generally depicted in art as being a young and beardless man.

✠

length but was denounced as a blasphemer, taken out of the city, and stoned to death. His invocation by headache sufferers is by association with the sharp pain of his stoning.

✠

c. 35 died
FEAST DAY: 26 December
CULT: Began in fourth
century or earlier; 415 relics
discovered at (?)Kafr Gamala,
translated to Constantinople
and later Rome; became
widespread in East and West;
invocation against headaches
emerged only in later
Middle Ages
OTHER PATRONAGE: Deacons
EMBLEMS: Stones; palm

✠

✠

Legend records that in the fifth century Stephen's body was taken to St. Laurence's tomb in Rome and that, as depicted here, Laurence moved aside to make room for Stephen.

✠

Stephen wears a deacon's robes in this painting of his martyrdom.

ABOVE *The New Testament describes how an angry mob dragged Stephen outside the city of Jerusalem and stoned him. The seated figure on the left in this engraving of Stephen's martyrdom is Saul, later St. Paul, who had agreed to his death.*

ABOVE RIGHT *Paintings of Stephen preaching traditionally show him outdoors and standing on a step or dais; often, as in this fresco by Fra Angelico, his listeners are women and children. He died because he accused the Sanhedrin of being obstinate and of betraying and murdering Christ.*

RIGHT *A French painting from a cartoon by Raphael; the New Testament records that just before Stephen died he fell on his knees and cried: "Lord lay not this sin to their charges."*

BLINDNESS
✛
LUCY
(died c. 304)

It is known that Lucy was a martyr at Syracuse, Sicily, probably during the persecution by Emperor Diocletian. Further details of her life are dramatic but largely legendary. She is portrayed as the daughter of wealthy and noble parents, a dedicated virgin who gave away her goods to feed the poor and refused all offers of marriage. On one occasion she tore out her eyes to discourage an admirer, but they were miraculously restored to her.

She was denounced as a Christian by a pagan suitor she had rejected and sentenced to prostitution in a brothel—but, by a miracle, she was made immovable and the guards could not take her there. Divine intervention also saved her from being burned to death. Finally her throat was cut with a sword.

Her name is connected with the Latin word for light, *lux*, and she is widely invoked for diseases of the eyes.

✛

The legend that Lucy tore her eyes out and sent them to a suitor to discourage his attentions is the reason why one of her emblems is two eyes on a platter. This sixteenth-century portrayal of the saint also shows her carrying the martyr's palm.

✛

✛
c. 304 died Syracuse, Sicily
FEAST DAY: 13 December
CULT: Early and widespread in East and West;
relics claimed by Venice
OTHER PATRONAGES: Glaziers; cutlers
ALSO INVOKED: Against hemorrhage;
throat infections
EMBLEMS: Two eyes on platter; sword; lamp
✛

DEAFNESS
✛
OUEN
(c. 600–684)

Born at Sancy, near Soissons, France, Ouen was chancellor to two Frankish kings, Lothar II and, from 629, Dagobert I. When he was about 36, however, Ouen left the court to found the Abbey of Rebais and took holy orders. In 641 he became bishop of Rouen. Although his involvement with politics

Ouen, as bishop of Rouen, uses his healing powers to restore hearing to deaf people.

✢

continued—he was advisor to Queen Bathild and later to Ebroin, the future ruler of the Franks—he was a zealous, reforming and missionary bishop, who founded monasteries and opposed the practice of buying and selling ecclesiastical preferments. At Rouen his relics were famed for their healing properties, in particular for restoring hearing to deaf people.

✢

c. 600 born Sancy, near Soissons; 636 founded Abbey of Rebais; 641 bishop of Rouen; 684 died Clichy
FEAST DAY: 24 August
ALSO KNOWN AS: Audoenus; Dado; Owen
CULT: Popular in England and France; Canterbury and Rouen claimed his relics in Middle Ages

✢

STOMACH TROUBLES
✢
WOLFGANG
(c. 924–994)

Wolfgang was a teacher, monk and bishop whose ability, learning and humility earned him the admiration of his contemporaries and who exercised a strong and valuable influence at the court of the Holy Roman Emperors. Educated at the Abbey of Reichenau on Lake Constance, he directed the cathedral schools at Wurzburg and Trier and, in 964, at the age of 40, became a monk at Einsiedeln (now in Switzerland). After an only partly successful mission to convert the Magyars in Pannonia (Hungary), he became bishop of Regensburg (now in Germany) in 972. Here he improved standards of discipline and learning amongst the clergy and monasteries.

A gifted preacher, he continued to live as a monk during the 22 years of his episcopate and to distribute alms to the poor, by whom he was known as the Great Almoner. He was tutor to the future emperor Henry II. On his death his cult sprang up at Regensburg, where many miracles of healing were recorded, notably of troubles of the stomach.

✢

c. 924 born Swabia; 964 monk at Einsiedeln; 972 bishop of Regensburg; 994 died Puppingen near Linz; 1052 canonized by Pope Leo IX
FEAST DAY: 31 October
CULT: Centered on Regensburg
EMBLEMS: Church; hatchet

✢

CANCER
✢
ALDEGONDA
(c. 635–684)

Aldegonda was born in Hainault to a devout family: both her parents, Walbert and Bertilia, and her sister, Walturdis, were later invoked as saints. She refused marriage and became an anchoress at Maubeuge (now in France) and, later, abbess of the monastery for monks and nuns that was founded there. She had many supernatural visions, and bore the agonizing pain of cancer of the breast with patience and fortitude, the reason she is invoked against cancer.

✢

c. 635 born in Hainault; 684 died Maubeuge
FEAST DAY: 30 January
ALSO KNOWN AS: Aldegun
ALSO INVOKED: Against childhood diseases; sudden death; wounds

✢

BREAST DISORDERS
✛
AGATHA
(?third century)

Agatha was martyred at Catania in Sicily, possibly in the third century. Legend casts her as a girl of good family who had taken vows of virginity. She rejected a high-ranking suitor, Quintinian; he indicted her as a Christian and handed her over to a wicked woman called Aphrodisia who, with her six daughters, kept a brothel. Agatha stood firm against their attempts to corrupt her, and Quintinian ordered her to be beaten and imprisoned. She was stretched on the rack and burned with torches, but remained cheerful throughout her ordeal. Quintinian then commanded her breasts to be crushed and cut off—the reason she is invoked against breast diseases—but they were

miraculously restored by St. Peter. Finally, Agatha was rolled naked over fiery coals and she died while being carried back to her dungeon.

✛

?Third century
FEAST DAY: 5 February
CULT: From fourth century; especially popular in Sicily
OTHER PATRONAGE: Bellfounders
ALSO INVOKED: Against fire; volcanic eruptions
EMBLEM: Breasts (often confused with loaves) in a dish; knife

✛

RHEUMATISM
✛
JAMES THE GREAT
(died 44)

With his brother St. John the Apostle, James was called on by Jesus to leave his life as a fisherman on the Sea of Galilee and become one of his disciples. He was one of the inner circle of Jesus' followers who

Scenes of Agatha's mutilation are rare in art; this one is from a fifteenth-century Swiss altarpiece.

James the Great wears a cockle shell and carries a pilgrim's staff; both are his emblems.

witnessed his transfiguration and agony in the garden of Gethsemane; and the first apostle to die for his faith—he was put to the sword in 44 on the orders of King Herod Agrippa, who wished to please the Jewish opponents of Christianity.

A seventh-century story that James preached the gospel in Spain is apocryphal, but his relics were claimed 200 years later by Santiago di Compostela, which became one of the great centers of pilgrimage in the West. Rheumatism was one of the many problems and illnesses which his relics were noted for curing.

---

44 died Jerusalem
FEAST DAY: 25 July
CULT: Widespread
EMBLEMS: Cockle shell; pilgrim staff; sword; key

CRAMP

✠

PANCRAS
(died c. 304)

Pancras was a Roman martyr buried on the Aurelian Way whose remains were the focus of an important cult. According to legend he was an orphan from Phrygia (Turkey). His father, a wealthy Christian, was killed for his faith during the Diocletian persecution and Pancras came to Rome with his uncle, Dionysius. Pancras was martyred by being beheaded, at the age of 14. His invocation against cramp derives from the story that a perjurer tried to swear falsely by touching Pancras' tomb, but the power of the saint froze his arm and he fell down dead.

---

c. 304 died Rome
FEAST DAY: 12 May
CULT: Centered on San Pancrazio Church, Rome;
England from seventh century
OTHER PATRONAGE: Children
ALSO INVOKED: Against headache; perjury;
false witness
EMBLEMS: Palm; sword; stone

St. Pancras Old Church in London was one of six early English churches dedicated to the saint.

BROKEN BONES

✠

STANISLAUS KOSTKA
(1550–1568)

Stanislaus was born in a castle in Rostkovo in Poland, the younger son of a Polish senator. In 1563, at the age of 13, his parents sent him to the Jesuit college in Vienna with his brother Paul and his tutor Bilinsky. Both were contemptuous of his dedication to the Jesuit way of life and Paul—who bullied and terrorized his younger brother—insisted, against Stanislaus' wishes, that the three of them lodge in a Lutheran household.

After two years Stanislaus fell ill, but his landlord refused to allow the Blessed Sacrament in the house and Stanislaus' life was saved only by his prayers to St. Barbara. On his recovery he vowed to become a Jesuit and when his family forbade this walked 350 miles to Rome. Here he was received into the order by Francis Borgia in 1567, when he was 17. Within a year Stanislaus was dead, but his reputation for angelic innocence, and the visions and ecstasies he experienced in Rome led to a cult arising around his remains. The fact that he bravely withstood savage bullying is the basis for his later invocation against broken bones.

✣

1550 born Rostkovo, Poland;
1563 went to Vienna to the Jesuit seminary;
1567 accepted into the order at Rome; 1568 died;
1726 canonized
FEAST DAY: 13 November

✣

PARALYSIS
✣
OSMUND
(died 1099)

A Norman follower of William the Conqueror, Osmund was first a royal chaplain and, in 1072, the king's chancellor. As bishop of Salisbury from 1078 until his death, he completed building the cathedral in Old Sarum, reorganized its chapter and was involved with the Domesday survey.

His miracles were many and varied, and gave rise to his invocation against a number of ills—the cure at his shrine in Salisbury cathedral of a paralyzed beggar named Simon is the reason why he is invoked against paralysis. Despite his efficacy his canonization process, started in 1228, took until 1456 to complete.

✣

Eleventh century born Normandy; 1072 chancellor
of England; 1078 bishop of Salisbury; 1099 died;
1456 canonized
FEAST DAY: 4 December
CULT: In England
ALSO INVOKED: Against toothache; rupture;
madness

✣

FEVER
✣
ANTONINUS OF FLORENCE
(1389–1459)

A member of the Pierozzi family of Florence, Antoninus joined the Dominican order there in 1405 when he was 16 and became prior of Cortona, and then, in 1418, of Fiesole. He served for a while in Rome and returned to Florence in 1435 where, with the financial help of Cosimo de Medici, he founded the friary of San Marco. This was decorated by Fra Angelico, who had been a novice with Antoninus, and became a center of Renaissance humanism.

In 1439 Antoninus was a prominent member of the council of Florence, convened to end the schism between the Eastern and Western Churches, and in 1446 he was appointed archbishop of Florence. He discharged his responsibilities in an exemplary fashion. He owned no horses, only a mule, and toured his diocese yearly, preaching, teaching and dispensing justice; he gave alms to the poor and helped the victims of plagues and earthquakes. He is said to have cured the sick—hence his invocation against fever—and was seen by Cosimo de Medici as the preserver of the republic of Florence.

Antoninus was also a distinguished writer on local and international law and on moral theology; one of his treatises went into more than 100 editions before 1500. An important theologian, Antoninus' abilities and judgment were greatly valued by church and state alike: in later life he acted as a diplomat on Florence's behalf and served on a committee reforming the papal court. He was canonized in 1523.

✣

1389 born Florence; 1405 became a Dominican
friar; 1418–28 prior of Fiesole; 1432–5 vicar-general
of the Dominicans of the Strict Observance in Rome;
1436 founded friary of San Marco, Florence;
1446 archbishop of Florence; 1459 died Florence;
1523 canonized
FEAST DAY: 10 May
CULT: Reduced to local status since 1969

✣

SNAKEBITE
✛
PAUL
(died c. 65)

Paul was a charismatic preacher, a powerful missionary, and a remarkable thinker whose theological and doctrinal ideas were of seminal importance to the Christian church in its formative years. Born at Tarsus in Cilicia (Turkey), and originally known as Saul, he was a Jew of the Pharisee sect and a Roman citizen, who became a tent maker by profession. At first a leading persecutor of Christians in Jerusalem—he was present at the stoning of St. Stephen and later sought out others and handed them over to the authorities—he experienced a vision of Christ on the road to Damascus and was converted to Christianity. After retreating for three years into the Arabian desert he returned to Damascus where his Jewish enemies threatened his life; he escaped by being lowered over the walls of the city in a basket.

Paul then traveled to Jerusalem and to Antioch, where he and St. Barnabas began their highly successful mission to the gentiles. In the years between 45 and 56 he went on several great missionary journeys—to Cyprus, Asia Minor, Macedonia and Greece—before returning to Jerusalem. Here his preaching against the Jewish law caused a riot and he was arrested. Paul invoked his right as a Roman citizen to be tried before the emperor Nero. This was granted, but after a voyage during which he was shipwrecked at Malta, he was put under house arrest for two years. Most authorities agree that he was tried and acquitted and traveled on missions to Ephesus and perhaps Spain, only to be beheaded during the persecutions of Nero.

Paul is invoked against snakebite because of the legend that a viper bit him in the hand without causing him any harm.

———————— ✛ ————————

Born Tarsus, Cilicia; converted to Christianity; c. 45 began his missionary journeys; c. 65 died Rome
FEAST DAY: 29 June
EMBLEMS: Sword; book

———————— ✛ ————————

On the road to Damascus Paul was flung to the ground and blinded by a vision of Christ; this sixteenth-century painting of his conversion is by Pieter Breughel the Elder.

A sixteenth-century Hungarian painting shows Paul holding both of his emblems: the sword with which he was beheaded on Nero's orders and a book, representing his authorship of his Epistles.

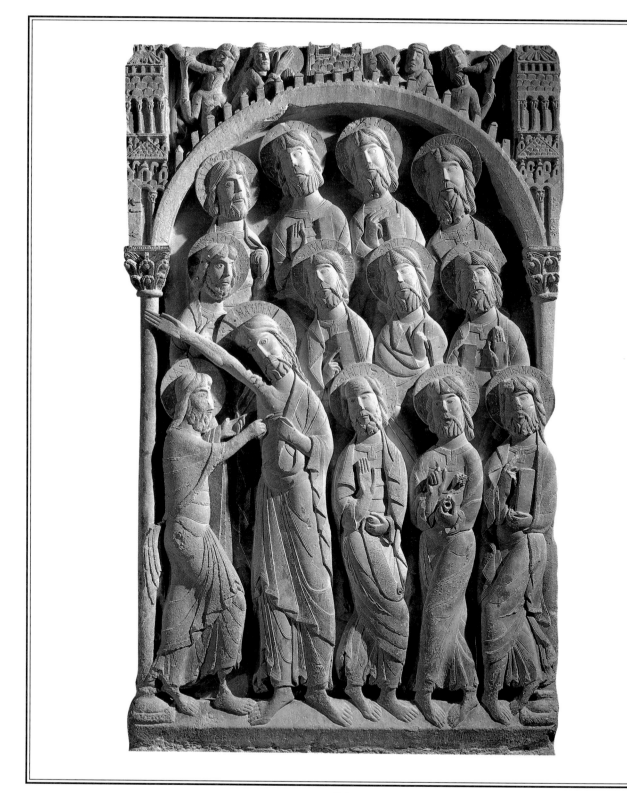

120

CHAPTER EIGHT

✛

ARTS AND CRAFTS

Sing unto the Lord with the harp.
PSALMS 98:5

———————— ✛ ————————

ARCHITECTS
✛
THOMAS
(first century)

Thomas the Apostle is mentioned in all the Gospels. He was prepared to die with Jesus, but later, after the Resurrection, refused to believe in the risen Christ until he had touched his wounds (hence the expression Doubting Thomas).

Little is known about the rest of his life. One tradition suggests that he was a missionary in Parthia. Another, far stronger one, records that he traveled to India, was killed with a spear and was buried near Madras, at Mylapore. An ancient cross still marks his supposed burial place, and the Syrian Christians on India's Malabar coast claim him as their founder, describing themselves as the ''St. Thomas Christians.''

His patronage of architects is based on a colorful tale in the apocryphal Acts of Thomas: an Indian king gave Thomas a large sum of money to build a palace, for which he had produced plans. Instead Thomas spent it on the poor, ''thus building a palace in heaven.''

———————— ✛ ————————

RIGHT Thomas, on the right in this wooden carving, is the patron saint of architects.

LEFT Watched by his fellow apostles, Thomas (page 121) satisfies himself that the figure before him is the risen Christ.

———————— ✛ ————————

First century; c. 72 died
FEAST DAY: 3 July
ALSO KNOWN AS: Didymus, the twin
CULT: Widespread in Middle Ages. Relics reputedly taken from Mylapore to Edessa (now Urfa, Turkey), then Chios in the Aegean Sea and Ortona, Italy
OTHER PATRONAGE: Builders
ALSO INVOKED: By the blind (because of his early spiritual blindness)
EMBLEMS: T-square; spear

———————— ✛ ————————

PAINTERS
✦
LUKE
(first century)

L uke, the evangelist, was a Greek doctor—St. Paul, whose disciple he became, described him as "our beloved Luke, the physician"—and may have been born in Antioch. His writings, the third Gospel and the continuation of the Acts of the Apostles, suggest that he traveled with Paul on some of his missionary journeys; Paul refers to Luke as his companion in three letters written from Rome.

There is a second-century tradition that Luke died, unmarried, in Greece at the age of 84; it is unlikely that he was martyred.

The much later tradition that he was an artist, the reason for his patronage of painters, is unfounded. However, his artistry with words has inspired numerous artistic masterpieces by others.

✦

First century
FEAST DAY: 18 October
OTHER PATRONAGES: Physicians; surgeons;
sculptors
EMBLEM: Winged calf (one of the symbols of the
four evangelists)

✦

POETS
✦
COLUMBA
(c. 521–597)

A leading saint of both Scotland and Ireland, Columba was born at Garton, Donegal, became a monk and priest at Gasnevin, and founded major monasteries in Ireland. In 565, when he was in his mid-40s, he left his homeland for Scotland. It is not clear if this was as a penance because of his moral

✦

Luke's patronage of painters is based on the tradition that he painted a portrait of the Virgin Mary, and variations on this theme were popular with Dutch and Flemish artists during the 15th and 16th centuries. This painting by Roger van der Weyden shows Luke drawing the Virgin and the infant Jesus.

✦

responsibility for a clan war—which climaxed in a battle in which 3,000 men were killed—or because of his missionary zeal to convert the Picts. Certainly, the monastery he and his companions founded at Iona (Holy Island) became the headquarters for missions to the Picts, Scots and Northumbrians.

Columba was the focal point of an upsurge in Celtic Christianity in northern Britain which was to spread south and, with the Celtic missionaries, to continental Europe. He is also credited with converting Brude, king of the Picts, and, in 574, with consecrating Aidan, the Irish king of Argyll.

Tall and athletic, with a voice that allegedly could be heard a mile away, Columba was also a fine poet and bard, some of whose work survives, and is thus a patron of poets. He was also a skilled scribe: the Cathach, a psalter he had written in his own hand, was later enshrined and used in battles to symbolize his power. The many miracles attributed to him include the killing of a dangerous wild boar by the power of his word, and driving a terrible monster away from Loch Ness by the efficacy of his prayers.

---

c. 521 born Donegal, Ireland; founded monasteries at Derry (546), Durrow (c. 556), (?)Kells; 565 went to Iona, Scotland; 597 died Iona; 849 relics translated to Dunkeld, Scotland
FEAST DAY: 9 June
ALSO KNOWN AS: Columcille
CULT: Strong in Scotland, Ireland and northern England; Dunkeld became a pilgrimage center

---

ACTORS AND COMEDIANS

GENESIUS
(died c. 303)

The legend of Genesius the Actor describes him as a comic actor who, while satirizing baptism during the performance of an anti-Christian play for Diocletian in Rome, was suddenly converted to the faith.

He declared himself to the emperor who, enraged, ordered his torture. Genesius refused to recant and was beheaded.

This tale, which is also told of three other actor-martyrs, was attached to the cult of Genesius of Arles, a genuine martyr. This Genesius was a notary and court official at Arles who, when instructed to put on public record a decree against Christians, declared that he was one himself, threw down his tablets, and fled from the court. He was pursued and martyred on the banks of the Rhône. A variant of this story made him a martyr in Rome and then became conflated with the story of Genesius the Actor. There is further confusion with the cult of Genesius of Clermont, a French bishop who died in c. 660.

---

c. 303 died Arles
FEAST DAY (for Genesius the Actor and Genesius of Arles): 25 August

---

WRITERS

JOHN THE APOSTLE
(died c. 100)

John and his brother James the Great were fishermen on the Sea of Galilee. They were summoned by Jesus as his disciples and called by him the "sons of thunder" because of their fiery temperaments. With St. Peter, they witnessed Jesus' transfiguration and agony at Gethsemane, and John is traditionally identified as "the disciple whom Jesus loved" at the Last Supper, the guardian of the Blessed Virgin Mary, and the first of the apostles to see the risen Christ.

He later ministered with St. Peter in Jerusalem and Samaria, and last appears in the New Testament as an exile on the island of Patmos. According to later ecclesiastical tradition he was in Rome at the time of Emperor Diocletian and escaped alive when he was boiled in a cauldron of oil.

John probably spent his last years at Ephesus (now an archaeological site in Turkey) where he died at a great age. Many anecdotes are told about his ministry

John is often shown writing the Fourth Gospel. In this fifteenth-century illustration an eagle, symbolizing his inspiration, is on his right.

El Greco portrays John carrying a chalice from which a snake is emerging—an allusion to the legend that the saint survived drinking from a poisoned cup.

in the city: the legendary challenge to him by a high priest of the Temple of Diana to drink from a poisoned cup as a test of his Christian faith—he did so and was unharmed; his fear that the baths would collapse because a heretic was bathing there; and his followers' eventual boredom with his frequent exhortations that they should love one another.

John's patronage of writers stems from his traditional but unprovable role as the author of the Fourth Gospel, three Epistles and the Book of Revelation.

---

c. 100 died (?)Ephesus
FEAST DAY: 27 December
OTHER PATRONAGES: Theologians; publishers
ALSO INVOKED: Against poisoning
EMBLEMS: Book; eagle; chalice; serpent

DANCERS

VITUS

(died c. 303)

Vitus was probably a martyr who died in southern Italy and whose remains were early associated with cures from sickness and possession by demons. Any real evidence about him is lost in layers of legend: that Vitus was converted to Christianity when he was seven; that with Modestus (his tutor) and Crescentia (his nurse) he fled to Lucania, and then Rome to escape persecution in Sicily; and that Vitus expelled the evil spirit that possessed Emperor Diocletian's son. Legend also records that when Vitus refused to renounce his faith he was cast into a boiling cauldron, only to emerge refreshed; and that a lion, sent to terrorize him, licked his feet. An angel eventually released Vitus and his companions and guided them back to Lucania, where they died.

His role as patron saint of dancers stems from his invocation by people suffering from Sydenham's chorea, a disease of childhood which produces involuntary jerking movements—since then known as St. Vitus' Dance.

died c. 303
FEAST DAY: 15 June
ALSO KNOWN AS: Guy
CULT: Early in southern Italy; Italy, France,
Germany, England in Middle Ages. Confined
to local status since 1969
OTHER PATRONAGES: Actors; comedians
ALSO INVOKED: Against dogbites; snakebites;
lightning; storms.
By people suffering from epilepsy

MUSICIANS
CECILIA
(?third century)

All that is known of Cecilia is that she lived in Rome, probably in the third century, founded a church in its Trastevere district, and was martyred and buried in the cemetery of St. Calixtus.

According to her colorful legend, she was an aristocratic Christian girl unwillingly betrothed to a pagan, Valerian. She sang to the Lord in her heart as the organs at her wedding feast were playing—hence her patronage of musicians—and refused to consummate the marriage. Instead she converted her bridegroom to her faith. He returned from his baptism to find Cecilia standing next to an angel who crowned both of them with roses and lilies.

Valerian's brother Tiberius also became a Christian and soon afterwards both brothers were imprisoned and condemned to death for the zealousness with which they buried the bodies of martyrs, and Cecilia was brought before the prefect. She obdurately refused to sacrifice to the Roman gods, converted her persecutors—400 people were baptized in her home—and was finally sentenced to death by suffocation in her bathroom. Although its furnace was fed with seven times the normal amount of fuel, Cecilia was unharmed, so beheading was tried. A soldier gave her three violent blows and she died slowly and in agony over the next three days.

?Third century
FEAST DAY: 22 November
ALSO KNOWN AS: Cecily; Celia
CULT: Widespread
EMBLEMS: Organ; lute; roses

The angel in this romanticized portrayal of Cecilia is holding the roses that are one of her emblems.

TV WRITERS
✛
CLARE OF ASSISI
(1194–1253)

Born into a noble family in Assisi, Umbria in Italy, Clare refused two offers of marriage and, at the age of 18, ran away from home to receive the veil from St. Francis of Assisi.

She was put in the care of the Benedictine nuns of Bastia until 1215, when with the help of St. Francis, she founded the Community of Poor Ladies (or Poor Clares). St. Francis provided her and a few companions with a house near the church of San Damiano at Assisi. Here, joined by Clare's mother and two sisters among others, they adopted a life of extreme poverty and asceticism according to the dictates of Francis.

The Poor Clares developed into an order which, like the Franciscan friars, their male counterparts, struck a chord with contemporary spiritual needs and spread rapidly throughout western Europe. The nuns adopted absolute poverty and lived entirely from alms. Although these were forthcoming in abundance, Clare, the order's abbess and leader for 40 years, steadfastly resisted any relaxation in its austerity—and even refused Pope Gregory IX's offer of a yearly revenue. She remained at Assisi all her life, fasting, wearing a hair shirt, going barefoot, and living as a contemplative. She was generous with alms to the poor of the town and when it was threatened with sacking by the armies of Emperor Frederick II, in 1243, she protected it by prayers and penances.

Despite severe illness—she was sometimes unable to get out of bed—she maintained her concern for Assisi and her nuns until her death in 1253 at the age of 60. She was canonized four years later.

Clare was named as the patron of television in 1958 because of a vision described by her biographer Thomas of Celano. One Christmas Day she was so ill that she was unable to attend Matins with her nuns. Lying alone in bed, she heard the service of Matins being celebrated in St. Francis' church, the harmonies of the singers and the swell of the organ, while at the same time seeing a vision of Jesus in the manger.

The Poor Clares' supper; Clare of Assisi is shown reading to her fellow nuns. The order's first convent was established in c. 1215.

✛

1194 born Assisi; 1213 became a nun; 1215 founded, with St. Francis, the Community of Poor Clares at Assisi; 1229 given the privilege of poverty by Pope Gregory IX; 1253 died; 1257 canonized
FEAST DAY: 11 August (formerly 12 August)
CULT: From the thirteenth and fourteenth centuries in Spain, Bohemia, France and England
OTHER PATRONAGE: Embroiderers
EMBLEM: Monstrance (commemorating her prayers for the city in 1243)

✛

SINGERS

✛

GREGORY THE GREAT
(c. 540–604)

Pope Gregory the Great was a commanding figure: a great statesman, a distinguished theologian and father of the medieval papacy. The son of a wealthy and pious Roman senator, he became prefect of the city—its highest civil office—when he was about 30. A year later, however, he decided to devote himself to God. He sold many of his substantial estates and founded six monasteries in Sicily and one—his own home, under the patronage of St. Andrew—in Rome. Here he retired as a monk to dedicate himself to a life of fasting and contemplation. In 585 he became advisor to Pope Pelagius, whom he succeeded in 590.

Gregory the Great was one of the Church's most influential writers.

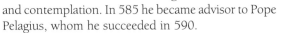

Gregory faced many problems. Rome was suffering from famine exacerbated by plague, he restructured the administration of the papal estates and used money from their income to counteract the effects of poverty and pestilence. The Lombards had invaded Italy in 568 and were ravaging the peninsula; Gregory negotiated a peace treaty with them in 592.

He promoted missionary activity to convert the Lombards, and also sent missions to the Visigoths in Spain, the Franks in Gaul (now France) and the Anglo-Saxons in England. It is said that he had seen some English boys for sale in a slave market in Rome and had been impressed by their beauty, exclaiming that these were not Angles but angels. He appointed St. Augustine, one of the monks at St. Andrew's monastery, leader of the mission to England in 596 and provided reinforcements for him. The conversion of England was one of the great achievements of his pontificate.

The *Pastoral Care*, written by Gregory in c. 591 to explain the office and duties of a bishop, was translated into Greek during his lifetime, into Anglo-Saxon by Alfred the Great more than two centuries later, and became a key text for the medieval Church. Gregory also wrote many noted homilies and commentaries; these works earned him his place as one of the Doctors of the Church.

Gregory's role as patron saint of singers arises from his work on the liturgy: the Gregorian chant is named after him. He concerned himself with establishing a Latin liturgy and founded a school of singers in Rome; he composed a number of prayers.

Gregory suffered from poor health for much of his life and in his last years was afflicted by gout and gastritis. He died in 604 when Rome was once more in the grip of plague and famine. His description of himself as "servant of the servants of God" illustrated his own humility; the use of this expression by all popes since reflects his key position in the history of the papacy and Western Church.

✛

c. 540 born Rome; c. 572 prefect of Rome;
573 founded monasteries in Sicily and Rome;
590 elected pope; 596 sent mission to England;
604 died Rome
FEAST DAY: 3 September
CULT: Early and widespread
ALSO INVOKED: Against plague
EMBLEMS: Crozier; dove; tiara

✛

ABOVE LEFT *A Byzantine ikon of Gregory the Great; he was greatly respected in the Eastern church.*

ABOVE *This fourteenth-century statue of Gregory shows him wearing the papal tiara, one of his emblems.*

LEFT *To end an epidemic of the plague that was raging in Rome, Gregory ordered the people to do penance by taking part in a procession through the city.*

RIGHT *Gregory at work; his crozier is in the background and a white dove, symbolizing the Holy Ghost, hovers above him.*

GOLDSMITHS
✚
DUNSTAN
(909–988)

Monk, counselor to the kings of Wessex and archbishop of Canterbury, Dunstan was one of the outstanding figures of tenth-century England. He was born into a noble Wessex family near Glastonbury in 909, educated at the abbey there and joined the court of King Athelstan. In 935 he was expelled as a magician. Dunstan nearly got married, but instead

Dunstan was a powerful influence on the Wessex kings, but eventually retired from court life.

took monastic vows and lived as a hermit near Glastonbury, where he excelled at the crafts of metalwork—the basis for his patronage of goldsmiths—bell-founding, illumination and needlework.

Four years later, in 939, Athelstan's half-brother, Edmund, succeeded to the Wessex throne. He recalled Dunstan to court and, after narrowly escaping death at Cheddar Gorge in what is now Somerset, made him abbot of Glastonbury, with the task of restoring the lax monastic life there in accordance with the Rule of St. Benedict. Dunstan's work was interrupted by a period of exile in Ghent—allegedly for rebuking the youthful King Edwy—but from 957, under King Edgar, he became in succession bishop of Worcester (957), bishop of London (959) and archbishop of Canterbury (960). He instituted a program to revive the organization and spiritual life of the Church, and with his associates Oswald and Ethelwold, presided over the reform of several ancient abbeys, including Bath and Westminster. He also promulgated the *Regularis Concordia*, a rule book for the monastic life.

Dunstan's work survived an anti-monastic backlash after Edgar's death in 975, but in his later years he withdrew from court to concentrate on his diocese, his crafts and music—he was an accomplished harp player—and on his monks and school at Canterbury.

He was nearly 80 when he died in 988. Many miracles and prophecies were attributed to him during his lifetime and he became one of England's most important saints.

✚

909 born Baltonsborough, near Glastonbury;
939 abbot of Glastonbury;
955 in exile in Ghent;
957 bishop of Worcester; 959 bishop of London;
960 archbishop of Canterbury;
988 died Canterbury
FEAST DAY: 19 May
CULT: Immediate. Dunstan's relics were a matter of long-running dispute between Canterbury and Glastonbury
OTHER PATRONAGES: Jewelers; locksmiths
EMBLEMS: Pincers; gold cup

✚

MILLERS
✛
CATHERINE OF ALEXANDRIA
(apocryphal; allegedly fourth century)

The legendary Catherine was a learned and beautiful maiden of Alexandria—some sources describe her as being of royal birth—who made a public protest to the emperor Maxentius against the worship of idols. He commanded 50 philosophers to oppose her but, although she was only 18, she demolished their arguments and converted them to Christianity. The emperor had them burned alive in punishment when they admitted their failure.

Maxentius then tried to seduce

ABOVE *Catherine of Alexandria is often shown wearing a crown, symbolizing her royal birth.*
✛

her with an offer of marriage. Her refusal—she replied that she was already betrothed to Christ—resulted in a long beating and imprisonment, but during her captivity she was fed by a dove and saw a vision of Christ. She also converted the emperor's wife and 200 soldiers. Maxentius next tried to break her on a spiked wheel—the "catherine wheel"—but this disintegrated and some spectators were injured. When Catherine was finally beheaded, milk, not blood, flowed from her veins. This legend has no corroboration in contemporary sources. The wheel on which she was tortured gave rise to her patronage of millers, whose work is based on the wheel.

✛

Apocryphal; allegedly fourth century
FEAST DAY: 25 November
(suppressed in 1969)
CULT: Widespread throughout Europe
during Middle Ages.
Centered on St. Catherine on
Mount Sinai, now in Egypt;
Catherine's remains were said to have been
carried there by angels after her death.
Suppressed in 1969 (because based on fiction)
OTHER PATRONAGES: Young girls; philosophers;
nurses; the dying; wheelwrights; spinners
EMBLEM: Spiked wheel

✛

✛

BELOW *Catherine argues with the philosophers; they were converted—and later executed.*

RIGHT *This painting of Catherine of Alexandria's mystic marriage to Christ shows the saint receiving a ring from the infant Jesus—a popular theme in art.*

ABOVE *This modern statue of Catherine of Alexandria is in a Buckinghamshire church.*

LEFT *In this painting by Raphael, Catherine of Alexandria is leaning on the wheel that is her emblem.*

According to legend, the wheel on which Catherine of Alexandria was sentenced to die was struck by a thunderbolt and broke apart. The saint was unharmed but a number of bystanders were hurt. Catherine was beheaded and angels carried her body to Mount Sinai where a church and monastery were later built.

LES CORPS D'ÉTAT & LEURS Sts PATRONS · Maréchal ferrant

SAINT ✠ ELOI

Serruriers

Chaudronniers

JEWELERS
✠
ELOI
(c. 588–660)

Eloi, shown here in a bishop's vestments, was a goldsmith, and master of the Frankish mint, for much of his life. After his death he was invoked on behalf of sick horses, hence the two other patronages—of farriers and blacksmiths—depicted in this illustration.

✠

Eloi was born at Chaptelat, near Limoges, into a Gallo-Roman family. His father was an artisan and apprenticed his young son to a goldsmith, the master of the mint at Limoges. Here Eloi developed outstanding skills as a jeweler and metalworker and learned how to use valuable and expensive materials with economy. Commissioned to make a throne for the Frankish king, Lothar II, he made two with the gold that was supplied and found a very high degree of favor with Lothar who appointed him master of the mint, and with his successor King Dagobert I.

Eloi produced many fine chalices, crosses, shrines and plaques—a number of pieces said to be his work have survived—and used the wealth he earned to found the monastery of Solignac and a convent in Paris. His outstanding skill in metalwork is the basis of his patronage of jewelers.

In 640, when he was in his mid-50s, Eloi resigned as master of the mint and was ordained priest. He was appointed bishop of Noyon the following year. Eloi was as successful as a churchman as he had been as a craftsman. He strove to stamp out pagan superstitions, and he launched important and successful missions to the pagan Frisians. As a counselor of the queen regent Bathild, formerly an Anglo-Saxon slave, he legislated for the rights of slaves to rest on holy days.

This depiction of Eloi at work as a farrier is based not on his life but on his patronage of horses. According to legend he was once forced to cut off the leg of a troublesome horse in order to shoe it—but later restored it.

---

c. 588 born Chaptelat near Limoges, France;
632 founded monastery of Solignac;
641 bishop of Noyon;
660 died Noyon
FEAST DAY: 1 December
ALSO KNOWN AS: Eligius
CULT: Popular throughout Europe by
later Middle Ages
OTHER PATRONAGES: Blacksmiths; farriers;
goldsmiths
EMBLEMS: Horseshoe; hammer;
pincers (with which he leads the devil
by the nose)

RIGHT Little is known about Bartholomew, but artists have generally portrayed him as bearded and middle-aged. He almost invariably holds the knife that was used to flay him alive.

TANNERS
BARTHOLOMEW
(first century)

One of Jesus' disciples, Bartholomew is often identified with Nathaniel in St. John's Gospel, whom Jesus described as "an Israelite, in whom there is no guile." Nothing else is known of him, although later traditions suggest that he preached in Asia Minor, northern India, and in Armenia, where he was flayed alive and then beheaded—the basis for his patronage of tanners.

First century
FEAST DAY: 24 August
CULT: Widespread; popular in England from
eleventh century when Canterbury cathedral
received an arm; relics allegedly previously passed
from Lipara to Beneventum, then to the Church of
St. Bartholomew in Rome
EMBLEM: Tanner's knife

LEFT *Crispin and Crispinian were shoemakers by trade but refused payment from their customers unless it was offered to them. The people of Soissons were so impressed by their way of life— they worked at night and preached the gospel during the day—that the brothers were able to make many converts.*

BAKERS
✦
HONORATUS
(late sixth century)

Honoratus is a shadowy figure. Bishop of Amiens in the late sixth century, all that is known of him is that he was born, and died, at Port-le-Grand in Ponthieu, France, and that he translated and celebrated the bones of St. Fuscianus and other saints. He is the patron of bakers because of a miracle attributed to him: during the mass the hand of God appeared above the chalice and held out a loaf of bread. His own cult was localized until his relics were translated in 1060: many miracles followed and he became known throughout France.

The church of Saint-Honoré in Paris was dedicated to him in 1204; and the city's Faubourg and rue Saint-Honoré are both named after him.

✦
Late sixth century
FEAST DAY: 16 May
CULT: Localized until Honoratus' relics were translated in 1060
ALSO KNOWN AS: Honorius
OTHER PATRONAGES: Confectioners
EMBLEM: Loaves
✦

COBBLERS
✦
CRISPIN AND CRISPINIAN
(died c. 286)

Crispin and Crispinian were probably Roman martyrs who died in the third century, and whose remains were brought to Soissons in France in the sixth century or earlier. In Soissons the legend grew up that they were brothers, missionaries from Rome, who preached during the day and, although they were noblemen, worked as shoemakers at night.

They were martyred by being beheaded on the orders of the emperor Maximian, but not before the official who was tormenting them had committed suicide—infuriated because the brothers had survived both drowning and boiling.

Their patronage of cobblers was widely recognized. A long-lived tradition in England had Crispin and Crispinian living as exiles from persecution in the village of Faversham, in Kent.

✦
c. 286 died Rome
FEAST DAY: 25 October
CULT: Popular during Middle Ages
OTHER PATRONAGE: Shoemakers
EMBLEMS: Shoe; cobbler's last
✦

*The martyrdom of Crispin and
Crispinian; nearly four centuries
after their death St. Eloi embellished
their shrine.*

WEAVERS AND DYERS

MAURICE
(died c. 287)

The legendary Maurice was the leader of the Theban Legion, a force of Christians recruited by the emperor Maximian to fight against the rebellious Gauls. When, near Lake Geneva, the emperor demanded that the army sacrifice to the pagan gods for success, the Theban Legion refused to do so and fell back to Agaunum (now Saint-Maurice-en-Valais in Switzerland). Maximian killed one man in ten, then repeated the decimation. When the soldiers, encouraged by Maurice, still refused to yield, he ordered the massacre of the whole legion—more than 6,000 men.

Maurice—who was probably a genuine martyr—is usually portrayed as a native African, riding a horse. The reasons why he and his companions are patrons of weavers are obscure. Their portrayal on two famous sets of tapestries, at Saint-Maurice in Vienne (France) and Saint-Maurice at Angers, may have forged the connection.

---

c. 287 died Agaunum (Saint-Maurice-en-Valais)
FEAST DAY: 22 September
CULT: Widespread, especially in Austria,
northern Italy and Sardinia
OTHER PATRONAGE: Soldiers

STONEMASONS

FOUR CROWNED MARTYRS
(died ?306)

Two quite separate groups of martyrs are associated with the Four Crowned Martyrs. The less credible story tells of four Roman soldiers who refused to sacrifice to Aesculapius and were flogged to death.

The better tradition names them as Claudius, Nicostratus, Simpronian and Castorius, four Persian sculptors and masons of great talent—hence their patronage of stonemasons. A fifth martyr, Simplicius, is ignored, possibly owing to the fact that he became a Christian simply because he thought his colleagues' skills at carving stemmed from their religion. Their work was much valued by Diocletian, but when they refused to carve an image of the god Aesculapius for him he demanded that they sacrifice to the Roman gods. They refused because they were Christians.

The emperor then ordered an inquiry by Lampadius, a Roman officer, who died suddenly before it was completed. Lampadius' relatives blamed the masons for his death, and the martyrs were shut up in lead caskets and thrown into the river where they died.

?306 died Sirmium (near Belgrade)
FEAST DAY: 8 November
CULT: Widespread. Reduced to local status in 1969

POTTERS

JUSTA AND RUFFINA
(?third century)

According to legend, Justa and Ruffina were Christian sisters in Seville. They made their living selling earthenware pots, but refused to sell their wares to be used in ceremonies to honor the Roman gods. When a group of pagans smashed their stock, Justa and Ruffina retaliated by destroying a pagan idol. They were brought before Diogenes, governor of Seville, who, when they declared their Christianity, ordered that they should be tortured on the rack. Both refused to recant and Justa died on the rack. Ruffina was strangled. Although this tale is probably based on a real tradition there have been significant changes: in the earliest versions Justa is a man, Justus.

?Third century
FEAST DAY: 19 July
CULT: Widespread in Spain
OTHER PATRONAGE: Seville
EMBLEM: Pots

Justa and Ruffina hold earthenware pots—their emblem—in this painting by Goya. The sisters are also holding palm fronds, symbols of their martyrdom. In the background are the towers of Seville cathedral.

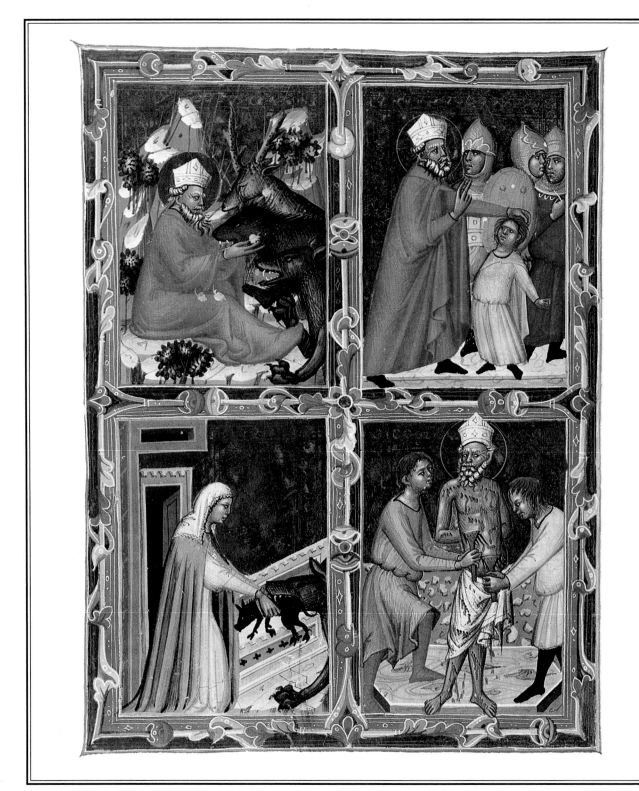

CHAPTER NINE

✛

THE ANIMAL KINGDOM

... every living thing that moveth upon the earth.
GENESIS 1:28

✛

WILD ANIMALS

✛

BLAISE
(died c. 316)

Little fact and much legend surround Blaise. Historically, he was said to have been a bishop of Sebasta in Armenia, who was martyred at the time of the emperor Licinius. Fictitious lives portray him as the son of wealthy parents, who was consecrated as bishop when a young man and fled persecution by hiding in a cave. Here he tended sick and wounded animals—the basis of his patronage of wild animals.

He also saved a young boy who was about to choke to death on a fishbone; when Blaise was later captured and imprisoned, the boy's mother gave him food and candles.

According to legend, Blaise's flesh was torn with wool combs before he was beheaded.

✛

c. 316 died
FEAST DAY: 3 February
CULT: Widespread from eighth century
OTHER PATRONAGE: Wool combers
ALSO INVOKED: Against diseases of the throat
EMBLEMS: Wool comb; two crossed candles

✛

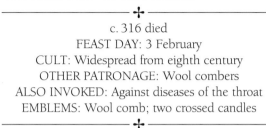

LEFT Episodes from the life of St. Blaise, patron of wild animals (page 141). They include the saint's final torture, when his flesh was torn with iron combs.

WOLVES

✛

EDMUND OF EAST ANGLIA
(841–869)

Of noble Christian descent, Edmund was chosen as king of the East Angles in 855 at the age of 14. When the pagan Danes invaded his kingdom in 869 he led an army against them; he was finally defeated and taken prisoner.

Edmund was martyred at Hellesdon, Norfolk, where, according to legend, he was tied to a tree, shot with arrows, and then beheaded. A wolf guarded his head after death and is thus one of his emblems.

A window in an Essex church depicts Edmund's death; according to legend he was killed when he refused to share his kingdom with pagans.

841 born; 855 king of the East Angles; 869 died
FEAST DAY: 20 November
CULT: Very popular in England; also in Toulouse
EMBLEMS: Wolf; arrow

LIONS

MARK

(died c. 74)

Mark was the author of the earliest of the four Gospels, for which he is said to have drawn upon the teachings of St. Peter. He is generally identified as the companion of Peter and Paul in the Acts of the Apostles, the son of a woman called Mary at whose house in Jerusalem the apostles met, and perhaps the young man who fled naked from Gethsemane when Christ was arrested there. Tradition relates that after missions in Cyprus and Rome he went to Alexandria, where he was martyred during Emperor Nero's reign. His relics were moved in 829 from Alexandria to Venice, whose patron saint he is.

The second-century theologian Irenaeus equated each of the four winged creatures in Revelation—the lion, the calf, the man and the eagle—with one of the evangelists. Mark's symbol was the lion.

c. 74 died
FEAST DAY: 25 April
CULT: Widespread
EMBLEM: Winged lion

Both these illustrations show a lion—Mark's emblem—and depict the saint with a book, his attribute as one of the Four Evangelists.

LAMBS
✛
JOHN THE BAPTIST
(died c. 30)

Called in the Bible "the voice crying in the wilderness" and "the man sent from God," John the Baptist was said by Jesus to have been the greatest of all the prophets. According to the New Testament, he was born to Elizabeth, cousin of the Blessed Virgin Mary, and Zachariah, a temple priest, in their old age, an event that had been foretold by an angel.

In about 27 John began preaching in the wilderness of Judaea, and baptizing his followers—including Jesus himself—in the River Jordan. His message was that people should repent because the kingdom of heaven was at hand.

John's public criticism of Herod

An emaciated John the Baptist is shown carrying the Lamb of God.

✛

Antipas for his incestuous marriage to Herodias, his brother's wife, resulted in his imprisonment. He was executed without trial because of a trick: when Salome, Herodias' daughter, had delighted Herod by her dancing he agreed to grant her any wish. At the urging of her mother she insisted on receiving the head of John the Baptist. This was duly granted to her.

In the New Testament John hails Jesus as the Lamb of God, a reference to Isaiah's image of the lamb led to the slaughter to bear the sins of mankind, and perhaps also to the Jewish custom of sacrificing a lamb at Passover. This image was taken up in apostolic writings and by the Church, and St. John the Baptist is frequently depicted holding a lamb.

✛

c. 27 began preaching; c. 30 died Machaerus; buried
Sebaste, Samaria
FEAST DAY: 29 August
CULT: Widespread in East and West
OTHER PATRONAGES: Baptism; the monastic life;
the Knights Hospitaller
EMBLEMS: Lamb; slender cross

✛

This illustration from a Book of Hours shows John the Baptist in the wilderness—a subject that has been popular with artists through the centuries. A lamb—his emblem—is at his feet.

LEFT *John the Baptist exhorts his listeners to repent in this painting by Pieter Breughel the Younger. John foretold the coming of Christ, and described him as one who would baptize with the 'Holy Ghost and with fire.'*

BELOW LEFT *This late 16th-century portrayal of John the Baptist preaching to the multitude shows him standing in a makeshift pulpit. His ascetic life in the desert, where locusts and honey were his only food, was an inspiration to many early Christians.*

LEFT *The baptism of Christ, depicted in stained glass. The long, slender cross that John the Baptist holds in his left hand is one of his emblems. The white dove hovering above Jesus' head represents the Holy Ghost.*

BELOW *A nineteenth-century painting of John the Baptist's execution. He was beheaded at the request of Salome, Herod's step-daughter, and his head was brought to her on a large, flat dish. John's disciples collected and buried his body immediately afterwards.*

COWS

✛

PERPETUA
(died 203)

Perpetua was one of a group of early Christian martyrs whose heroic deaths at Carthage in North Africa were carefully documented by their contemporaries. A young married woman and the mother of a baby son, she was arrested while awaiting baptism. With her was another woman—the pregnant slave girl Felicitas—and four men including Revocatus, husband of Felicitas. Perpetua and her companions were at first under house arrest and were baptized during this period. Later they were thrown into prison, tried and condemned to be killed in the amphitheater by wild beasts.

While they were awaiting this fate one of the men, Secundulus, died; Felicitas gave birth to a daughter who was adopted by Christian friends; and Perpetua experienced a series of remarkable visions in which she vanquished the devil. She approached her death in a state of ecstasy. While the three remaining men, Satyrus, Saturninus and Revocatus, were mauled by leopards, boars and bears, Perpetua and Felicitas were attacked by a crazed cow—Perpetua's emblem in art. Severely wounded, the martyrs were finally killed by the gladiators' swords.

✛
---

203 died
FEAST DAY: 7 March
CULT: Widespread throughout the Church
EMBLEM: Cow

✛

HORSES

✛

HIPPOLYTUS
(died ?235)

Most accounts of Hippolytus' life are as much conjecture as fact. However, most authorities agree that he was born in the eastern Empire, and traveled to Rome where he became a leading writer (in Greek) on Christian theology and worship and a harsh critic of anyone who did not uphold his rigorous standards. In 217, when he censured Pope Calixtus I for being too lenient in disciplinary and doctrinal matters, his hard-line followers elected him the first of many antipopes.

The schism continued for 15 years and three pontificates until 235, when Hippolytus and his rival Pope Pontian were both sentenced to death by the anti-Christian emperor Maximinus. They were sent to the penal colony in Sardinia and died there, but not before they had been reconciled, ending the schism. Their remains were brought back to Rome by Pope Fabian a year later and were given a solemn burial.

Within a few decades of his death Hippolytus was confused with a mythical companion of St. Laurence who, like Hippolytus, son of Theseus in Greek mythology, was killed by wild horses. As a result, in the Middle Ages St. Hippolytus was associated with the protection, and curing, of horses.

✛

?Before 170 born; ?217–35 antipope; ?235 died
FEAST DAY: 13 August
EMBLEM: Horses

✛

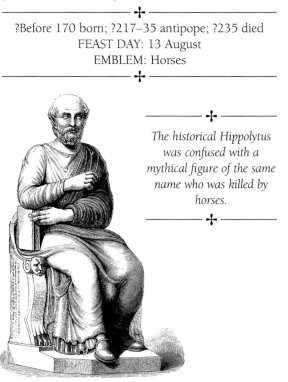

✛

The historical Hippolytus was confused with a mythical figure of the same name who was killed by horses.

✛

SWAN
✤
HUGH OF LINCOLN
(c. 1140–1200)

Hugh of Lincoln is one of the most attractive of all medieval saints. Born in Avallon, Burgundy, he was educated and professed by the Augustinian canons of Villarbenoît. In his mid-twenties he moved across to a more ascetic life at the monastery of the Grande-Chartreuse where, within a decade, he rose to the office of procurator. He also came to the notice of Henry II, king of England, and in c. 1180 Henry invited Hugh to revivify his ailing Carthusian foundation at Witham, Somerset.

Hugh began by insisting that the king should compensate the villagers turned out of their houses to make way for the monastery, and over the next six years transformed it into a flourishing foundation. In 1186 Henry appointed him bishop of Lincoln, the largest diocese in England. He was an outstanding spiritual leader in the diocese and an effective politician outside. Fearless in the face of Plantagenet rages, he upheld the rights of the Church against royal officials and refused to pay unjust dues to the Crown. He organized the rebuilding of Lincoln cathedral, held synods and councils, made regular visitations in his diocese and acted as the pope's representative in several major canon law cases. During a riot in Lincoln he intervened on behalf of the Jews; and he personally tended lepers and the sick.

Hugh's affection for his pet swan—a wild bird which lived at his manor of Stow near Lincoln—is vividly described by contemporary chroniclers. For 14 years the bird predicted his visits by its animated behavior, followed and protected him while he was staying at Stow, and returned to the wild on his departure. On Hugh's last visit, in 1200, the swan is said to have anticipated his impending death. It outlived him by many years and became his emblem.

✤

c. 1140 born Avallon, Burgundy; c. 1164 joined the Carthusian monastery of the Grande-Chartreuse; c. 1180 prior of Witham, Somerset; 1186 bishop of Lincoln; 1200 died London; 1220 canonized
FEAST DAY: 17 November
CULT: England in the thirteenth century; France, Italy, Spain, Germany, Flanders in the fourteenth century
EMBLEMS: Swan; chalice

✤

Lincoln cathedral, rebuilt after an earthquake in 1185.

DOGS
✤
HUBERT OF LIÈGE
(died 727)

The first bishop of Liège, Hubert was a pioneering missionary in the remote forests of the Ardennes. Details of his early life are obscure. According to legend he was converted while hunting on Good Friday, by seeing the image of Christ crucified between the

A modern church window in honor of Hubert of Liège.

✛

antlers of a stag; but it is known that he succeeded St. Lambert as bishop of Maastricht in 705. Eleven years later he moved his headquarters—and Lambert's relics—to Liège. From here he ran his missions to the pagans. He had an accident while fishing on the River Meuse, in 726, and died the next year.

An enthusiastic huntsman, Hubert became the patron saint of hunters and trappers in the Middle Ages, and his protection of healthy dogs is connected with this patronage.

✛

705 bishop of Maastricht; 716 moved to Liège;
727 died
FEAST DAY: 30 May
CULT: Immediate and widespread
OTHER PATRONAGES: Hunters; trappers
ALSO INVOKED: Against hydrophobia (rabies)
EMBLEM: Stag

✛

BEES
✛
AMBROSE
(339–397)

Ambrose—with Augustine, Jerome and Gregory the Great one of the four original Doctors of the Church—is often known as "the honey-tongued

doctor" and his emblem is a beehive, symbolizing his eloquence as a preacher and teacher. According to legend, he was unharmed when, as a child, a swarm of bees settled on him. Although the Ambrosian chant cannot be attributed to him with any certainty, he composed many hymns and wrote doctrinal and pastoral works with a practical slant.

Ambrose was the son of a Roman nobleman and was born in Trier, Germany, in 339. A successful lawyer, he became governor of Aemilia and Liguria in 370. When the bishop of Milan, the capital of the province, died four years later Ambrose, then in his mid-30s, was called to the cathedral to ensure the peaceful election of a new bishop—but to his great surprise found himself acclaimed and elected instead. He accepted only with reluctance; although a professed Christian, he was still awaiting baptism.

Milan was the administrative hub of the western Roman Empire and as its bishop, Ambrose was drawn

Scenes from a medieval Life of Ambrose.

into the political arena. He prevented a group of senators from restoring a statue of the goddess of Victory to the senate house in Rome, and refused to hand over a church to the heretical Arian Christians of Milan. He persuaded the emperor Maximus to split the western Empire with Valentinian II; and in 390 bravely reproved a later emperor, Theodosius, for ordering a massacre at Thessalonica in reprisal for the death of the governor. Theodosius submitted to a public penance for this misdeed. Ambrose's other emblem, a scourge, represents this penance.

---

339 born Trier, Germany; 374 elected bishop of Milan;
397 died Milan
FEAST DAY: 7 December
EMBLEMS: Beehive; scourge

BLACKBIRD
KEVIN
(died c. 618)

All the accounts of Kevin's life were written at least four centuries after his death, to enhance the reputation of the Irish Abbey of Glendalough. Although they contain much invention they are imbued with a feeling for natural beauty, and may be based on fact. They suggest that Kevin was born to a noble, formerly royal, family and was educated by monks—perhaps by St. Petroc of Cornwall who was reputedly in Ireland at that time. Having been ordained, Kevin settled as a hermit by the lake of Glendalough, where he attracted many followers and founded a monastic community which became not only one of the most important in Ireland but also a major pilgrimage center.

According to tradition Kevin—who is said to have lived to the age of 120—had a great love of nature. He fed his early followers on salmon caught for them by an otter; and when a blackbird laid its egg in his outstretched hand he maintained this position until it hatched. This scene is frequently represented in art.

---

c. 618 died
FEAST DAY: 3 June
ALSO KNOWN AS: Coemgenus (Latin);
Caoimhghin (Irish)
CULT: Widespread in Ireland
EMBLEM: Blackbird

DOVE
DAVID
(died ?601)

St. Davids, in the west of Wales, is named after the only Welsh saint to be recognized widely in the Western church. It was in this remote place—known formerly as Mynyw—that David founded a Celtic monastic community which followed a very austere rule and produced numerous saints.

Beyond this, little is known of him. According to the earliest surviving description of his life, which dates from almost five centuries after his death and is largely propaganda, he was the son of a Northern Welsh chieftain who founded 12 monasteries, including Mynyw and Glastonbury. It also records that he made a pilgrimage to Jerusalem where he was consecrated bishop and that he took part in two major councils of the Celtic church in Wales, at Cardigan and at Brefi (c. 545) where his fame as a preacher, holy man and worker of miracles was so great that he was recognized as the primate—the leading bishop—of Wales, and later its patron saint.

David modeled his way of life on that of the desert monks of Egypt, subsisting on a diet of vegetables, bread and water and practicing austerities such as immersing himself in cold water for many hours. His nickname, "the Waterman," could reflect his total abstinence from alcohol. He died at Mynyw and was buried there in about 601.

David is represented in art with a dove on his shoulder, evoking the legend that when he was asked to speak at the synod of Brefi the ground under his feet rose up, enabling him to be seen, and a snow-white dove—his emblem—perched on his shoulder, miraculously allowing his voice to be heard by everyone who was present.

?601 died at Mynyw (St. Davids)
FEAST DAY: 1 March
CULT: 1120 approved by Pope Calixtus II
ALSO KNOWN AS: Dewi (David is the closest English equivalent)
EMBLEM: Dove

BIRDS

GALL
(died c. 630)

Although Gall remained a hermit-monk and was never an abbot or bishop, he was a pioneer of Christianity in what is now Switzerland. Born in Ireland, he became a monk at Bangor, an important Irish monastery and the center of missions to Europe. In 585 he went with St. Columbanus—another Irish monk—to France, where he helped him to found the Abbeys of Annegray and Luxeuil.

In 610, when Columbanus was exiled for refusing to bless the illegitimate sons of the Frankish king Theoderic, Gall again accompanied him, this time to Switzerland.

Two years later Columbanus left for Italy, where he founded the Abbey of Bobbio, possibly after a disagreement with Gall, whom he considered insufficiently motivated in his missionary work.

Gall was later offered a bishopric by the Frankish king, Sigebert, and the abbacy of Luxeuil, but turned both down, preferring to remain a hermit and preacher and to teach by example. He is traditionally called upon to protect geese and poultry.

His connection with birds also emerges in the legend that a certain Duke Gunzo asked him to exorcize his daughter, who was possessed by evil spirits. Two bishops had already tried and failed, but Gall was successful: the spirits flew out of the girl's mouth in the form of a black bird.

Late sixth century born Ireland; c. 630 died near Bregenz, Switzerland
FEAST DAY: 16 October
ALSO KNOWN AS: Gaaech, Gilianus
CULT: Centered on his relics at Abbey of St. Gall
EMBLEM: Birds

FISH

NEOT
(died c. 877)

St. Neot's connection with fish is part of a rich series of legends about him which grew up more than two centuries after his death. The real Neot may have been a monk of Glastonbury who became a hermit in Cornwall and founded a small monastery near Bodmin Moor, at a place now named after him (St. Neot).

The legendary Neot was a very small man, so short that he had to stand on a stool when saying mass. He was also a close associate of Alfred the Great and advised him on military matters and education. More fancifully, he yoked stags to the plough to replace stolen oxen. The reason that his emblem is a fish lies in the legend that an angel showed him a supply of fish in a well which, as long as one was eaten each day, would never run out.

---

c. 877 died
FEAST DAY: 31 July
CULT: Popular in Cornwall
EMBLEM: Fish

SALMON

KENTIGERN
(died c. 612)

Kentigern, known also as Mungo (darling), is believed to have been born in Lothian in Scotland, and to have been a hermit-monk and missionary who was consecrated as the first bishop of the Britons of Strathclyde. He was driven away by persecution and as a result became a missionary, first in Cumbria and, later, perhaps in North Wales. He eventually returned to Glasgow where he again served as bishop, died—according to one biography at the unlikely age of 185—and was buried.

His emblems, a ring and a salmon, are displayed on the heraldic arms of Glasgow. This stems from a legend in which the queen of Strathclyde gave her royal husband's ring to her lover. The king, discovering this infidelity, repossessed the ring and secretly threw it out to sea, then ordered the queen to return it to him. She asked Kentigern for help, and one of his monks miraculously caught a salmon which had swallowed the ring. The saint was thus able to rescue the queen.

---

c. 612 died
FEAST DAY: 13 January
CULT: In Scotland and Cumbria; Glasgow cathedral claims his relics
ALSO KNOWN AS: Mungo
EMBLEMS: Salmon; ring

WHALES

BRENDAN THE NAVIGATOR
(c. 486–575)

A priest and monk, Brendan was born into and lived during the great flowering of Celtic Christianity that took place from the fifth to the seventh centuries. He is said to have spent his early childhood in the care of Ita, abbess of a community in County (Co) Limerick, Ireland, whose precepts were "Faith in God with purity of heart; simplicity of life with religion; generosity with love."

He was educated by another saint—Erc, bishop of Kerry—and during his long life is reputed to have paid visits to Columba, the charismatic missionary to the Picts in Scotland, and to Malo who had left his British home to preach the gospel in Brittany.

Some fact and a great deal of fiction are interwoven

in the accounts of Brendan's life. It is known that he lived and worked mainly in western Ireland, and that he founded Clonfert monastery, of which he was abbot, in c. 559. But his fame rests on the mythical adventures later described in *Brendan's Voyage*. This tenth-century romance tells of how Brendan and a company of monks sailed westwards over the Atlantic Ocean to a land of promise—sometimes identified as the Canary Islands, but more likely to be wholly imaginary. The exploits of the company are described. One of the most remarkable—and the reason for Brendan's association with whales—was their landing on the back of a sleeping whale, which they thought was an island, to celebrate mass at Easter. After the mass they lit a fire and started to prepare a banquet, but the great creature awoke from its slumbers and began to move, to the terror of the sailors; they rushed in haste to their ships and fled.

---

c. 486 born Co Kerry; foundations include Clonfert, Co Galway (c. 560); Annadown, Co Galway; Inishadroon, Co Clare; Ardfert, Co Kerry
FEAST DAY: 16 May
CULT: Ireland from the ninth century; Wales; Scotland; Brittany (tenth century)
EMBLEM: Whale

Brendan and his companions land on a whale in the belief that it is an island.

CHAPTER TEN
✛
CRISES AND DANGERS

For the great day of his wrath is come.
REVELATION 6:17

✛

WAR
✛
ELIZABETH OF PORTUGAL
(1271–1336)

The daughter of Peter III, king of Aragon, Elizabeth was only 12 when she was married to King Denis of Portugal. Ten years her senior, he was a capable ruler but a neglectful and unfaithful husband. Elizabeth bore him two children; then, at the age of 20, she turned to a life of piety, founding an orphanage, a hospital, and a home for abused women. She also provided hospitality for pilgrims and the poor. When her son Alfonso led an armed revolt against his father in 1320, she tried to mediate, but was banished for a time by her husband who suspected her motives.

Denis died in 1325 after a severe illness, and Elizabeth, then in her 50s, retired to Coimbra as a Franciscan tertiary and devoted herself to the poor and sick. But in 1336 her peacemaking skills—the reason she is invoked against war—were called upon again when her son, by now King Alfonso IV of Portugal, waged war against Alfonso XI of Castile. Elizabeth reconciled the two sides. But she exhausted herself doing so and died before she could return home. She was buried in the Poor Clares' convent at Coimbra and many miracles were reported at her tomb.

✛

LEFT Geneviève, protectress against disasters (page 155), prays for help as the Huns besiege Paris.

✛

1271 born; 1284 married Denis, king of Portugal;
1325 on Denis's death retired to Coimbra;
1336 died Estremoz; 1626 canonized
FEAST DAY: 4 July
ALSO KNOWN AS: Isabel
EMBLEMS: Rose; beggar

✛

EARTHQUAKE
✛
GREGORY THE WONDERWORKER
(c. 213–c. 270)

Gregory was a remarkable missionary in Pontus (Neo-Caesarea), Asia Minor. When he took office as bishop he found only 17 Christians in the city, but on his death left only 17 pagans. Born of wealthy parents, he traveled to Caesarea in Palestine in 233, where he studied under Origen and was baptized. About four years later he returned to Pontus and in 238, at the age of 25, was appointed bishop.

Gregory carried out his missionary work in highly troubled conditions: the persecution of Emperor Decius (250) when he and his fellow Christians fled the city; an outbreak of plague; an invasion by the Goths. He nevertheless produced numerous theological works, and attracted many converts by popularizing the Christian festivals. One story told of him is that the statues of the emperors in Pontus were thrown down by an earthquake, and replaced on his orders by holy images. He was also known as a healer of the sick and a visionary who communicated with the Blessed Virgin Mary. The many marvels and wonders attributed to him after his death include diverting the course of a river, draining a swamp and moving a mountain—elements that have led to his invocation against earthquake and flood.

---

c. 213 born Pontus, Asia Minor; 233 went to Caesarea, Palestine; c. 237 returned to Pontus; c. 238 elected bishop of Pontus; c. 270 died
FEAST DAY: 17 November
ALSO KNOWN AS: Gregory Thaumaturgus
CULT: Widespread but centered in Calabria and Sicily. Reduced to local status in 1969

View of Naples from the slopes of Vesuvius; the volcano still threatens the city today.

VOLCANIC ERUPTIONS
JANUARIUS
(died c. 305)

Januarius, bishop of Benevento, was martyred with six companions at Pozzuoli at the time of Emperor Diocletian; otherwise little is known of him.

His relics have been in Naples since 1497 and include what is supposedly a phial of his dried blood. Since 1389, with a few exceptions, this has allegedly become liquid three times a year, on each of the saint's feast days. One of these days is 16 December, an anniversary of the day when Januarius is said to have saved Naples from a volcanic eruption by Mount Vesuvius. He is still invoked for protection of Naples against the volcano.

---

c. 305 died at Pozzuoli
FEAST DAYS: 19 September; 16 December
ALSO KNOWN AS: Gennaro
OTHER PATRONAGE: Naples

Gregory the Wonderworker converts a pagan priest by causing a boulder to move through the air.

DISASTERS
✛
GENEVIÈVE
(c. 420–c. 500)

Born at Nanterre in France, probably to a noble family, Geneviève became a nun when she was about 15, and after the death of her parents moved to Paris. Here, with the support of St. Germanus of Auxerre who had known her since she was a child, she practiced a life of prayer, austerity and charitable works.

The Roman Empire in the west was by this time in terminal decline and the inhabitants of Gaul (now France) had little protection against the barbarians. In 451 the Huns, led by Attila, threatened Paris; Geneviève advised the citizens to stay in their homes and pray for deliverance. Attila and his band headed off to Orléans, and the city's escape was attributed to the efficacy of her prayers. This was the first of many occasions on which Geneviève saved Paris and Parisians—hence her cult as protectress from disasters.

Later, the Franks blockaded Paris, and she led a raiding party up the River Seine, to bring back corn from Troyes. Although the Frankish king was a pagan, he respected Geneviève and released captives at her request, as did his son Clovis. Clovis was baptized a Christian in 496 and founded the church of St. Peter and Paul. It later became the church of Sainte-Geneviève and is now the Panthéon. Geneviève was buried there after her death in c. 500.

✛

c. 420 born Nanterre; c. 435 became a nun and soon afterwards moved to Paris; c. 500 died Paris
FEAST DAY: 3 January
CULT: Ancient; spread in France, England and southern Germany in Middle Ages
OTHER PATRONAGE: Paris
EMBLEMS: Candle; bread; herd; keys

✛

ABOVE *In this eighteenth-century illustration the Virgin Mary is shown appearing to a young Geneviève, here portrayed as a shepherdess.*

LEFT *An angel helps Geneviève confront a demon.*

RIGHT *A romanticized, nineteenth-century painting of Geneviève as a child. The distaff she holds is an allusion to the tradition that she spent her early years tending sheep in Nanterre before leaving her home for Paris.*

BELOW *This sixteenth-century painting also depicts Geneviève as a shepherdess. According to tradition, she was seven years old when St. Germanus recognized her sanctity and encouraged her to take the veil as a nun.*

ABOVE *A nineteenth-century portrayal of Geneviève pleading with a pagan leader. She persuaded Childeric, king of the Franks, to release captives and gained both his respect and that of his son.*

LEFT *Paris today. Geneviève's prayers and counsel saved the city from the Huns in 451.*

PROTECTION FROM FIRE

✟

CATHERINE OF SIENA
(c. 1347–1380)

Catherine Benicasa was born at Siena in Tuscany, the 25th child of a wool-dyer. An attractive and lively girl, she had her first mystical experience when she was six, and resisted her parents' attempts to force her into marriage by cutting off the hair that was her chief beauty. Instead, she adopted a life of solitude, prayer and penance. In her early 20s she became a Dominican tertiary, and began to nurse the sick in hospital. A group of followers, known as the Caterinati, soon gathered round her and accompanied her on her many subsequent journeys, in Italy and to Avignon. Catherine was responsible for some spectacular conversions of evil-doers, and these and her important tracts and letters—dictated to her followers because she herself was illiterate—made her a prominent mystic and spiritual leader.

In 1374 she tended sufferers from a severe outbreak of plague in Siena. The following year she received the stigmata—the five wounds of Christ. They remained for the rest of her life, apparent only to herself while she lived but clearly visible after her death.

1375 was also the year in which she was drawn into politics. She tried to end a war between Florence and the Avignon papacy, and in the next year persuaded Pope Gregory XI to return the papal headquarters from Avignon to Rome. On his death in 1378 two rival popes were elected and Catherine supported the Roman pontiff, Urban VI, against Clement VII, his rival at Avignon. Intransigent by nature, she was openly critical of Urban. Nevertheless, she wore herself out by her stalwart work on his behalf and died in 1380, at the age of 33. She was canonized less than a century later, in 1461.

Catherine is invoked for protection against fire because of a striking miracle. Her sister left her in the kitchen sitting by the fire; when she returned Catherine was sitting in the fire itself from which she emerged wholly unscathed: not even her clothes were singed. Her biographer explained that the fire of holiness in her heart kept at bay the heat of the flames.

✟

c. 1347 born Siena; c. 1367 became a Dominican
tertiary and founded the Caterinati;
1375–80 involved in papal politics;
1380 died Rome; 1461 canonized;
1970 declared a Doctor of the Church
FEAST DAYS: 29 April (formerly 30 April)
CULT: Widespread
OTHER PATRONAGES: Siena; Italy (with St.
Francis)
EMBLEMS: Heart; lily; cross; stigmata

✟

COLD WEATHER

✟

SEBALD
(?eighth century)

Sebald, like many missionaries in eighth-century Germany, may have been an Anglo-Saxon. He is said to have lived as a hermit near Vicenza in Italy, and then to have traveled to Rome, from where Pope Gregory III sent him with St. Willibald into Bavaria. His date of death is not known, but by 1072 he had become the patron saint of Nuremberg.

A magnificent tomb in the city's sixteenth-century cathedral depicts his miracles. In one scene he fills an empty jug with wine from nowhere, in another he gives sight to a blind man.

The miracle of the icicles—the reason he is invoked against cold weather—is also depicted. Sebald is said to have taken refuge in a peasant's hovel. It was freezing cold and as there was no fuel of any kind in the house, he encouraged the woman of the house to throw icicles on the embers of the fire. She did so and they gave out great heat.

✟

?Eighth century
FEAST DAY: 19 August
OTHER PATRONAGES: Nuremberg; Bavaria

Sebald traveled to Rome from his hermitage in Vicenza; here he wears a pilgrim's robes.

BAD WEATHER

✛

MÉDARD
(c. 470–c. 560)

Born of a Frankish noble family in Picardy, Médard was in his 30s when he was ordained priest and 60 before he was appointed bishop of Vermand, a position he held until his death at the age of 90. He is said—probably erroneously—to have moved the headquarters of the see to Noyon to escape the raids of the Huns, and also to have been bishop of Tournai. He accepted as a nun the beautiful queen Radegonde, who had fled the intrigues of the Frankish court and her unfaithful husband Lothar and was to become one

An eagle rewarded Médard for a charitable act by sheltering him from a thunderstorm.

of France's most important saints. Medieval images of Médard show an eagle over his head sheltering him from the rain, the reason he is invoked against bad weather. It is also believed that the weather prevailing on his feast day will persist for a further 40 days.

✛

c. 470 born Salency, Picardy; c. 505 ordained priest;
c. 530 bishop of Vermand, and later of Noyon
and Tournai; c. 560 died
FEAST DAY: 8 June
CULT: Immediate
ALSO INVOKED: Against toothache

✛

LIGHTNING
✛
BARBARA
(?third to fourth century)

In legend Barbara was a maiden of extraordinary beauty whose father, Dioscorus, imprisoned her in a tower so that none of her many suitors could approach her. Here she converted, secretly, to Christianity—to the fury of her father who denounced her to the authorities. Barbara refused, even under torture, to renounce her faith, and Dioscorus was commanded to put her to death himself. He did so, and was straight away killed by a bolt of lightning, the reason why his daughter is invoked by those in danger of a similar fate.

It is possible that there was a real virgin-martyr Barbara, who was killed during the persecution of Emperor Maximian (c. 303), but her place of death is variously claimed to have been Egypt, Rome or Tuscany, and her date of death between 235 and 313.

✛

?Third to fourth century
FEAST DAY: 4 December
CULT: Popular in late Middle Ages,
particularly in France. Suppressed in 1969
OTHER PATRONAGES: Miners; gunners
ALSO INVOKED: For protection from sudden death
through cannon balls and subsiding mines
EMBLEMS: Tower; palm; cannon; chalice

✛

Barbara holds two of her emblems: the martyr's palm and the tower in which she was imprisoned.

RIGHT This painting on a fifteenth-century altarpiece shows Barbara's pagan father punishing her because of her conversion to Christianity.

✛

FLOODS
✛
FLORIAN
(died 404)

An officer in the Roman army, and an important official, Florian was martyred at Noricum (now in Austria) during Diocletian's reign. According to legend, he confessed his faith at Lorch when Aquilinus, the governor, was rounding up Christians.

He was scourged, flayed and finally drowned by being thrown into the River Enns with a stone round

his neck—the reason he is the patron saint of people in danger from floods. His body was later recovered and buried by a pious woman.

✛

404 died Noricum
FEAST DAY: 4 May
OTHER PATRONAGES: Linz, upper Austria;
those in danger from fire

✛

DROUGHT

✛

SWITHUN

(died 862)

Swithun was educated at the Old Minster, Winchester, the capital of Wessex, and became the chaplain and valued counselor of two kings of Wessex: Egbert (802–39) and Ethelwulf (839–58).

He was appointed bishop of Winchester in 852, and was noted for his charitable giving and for the many churches that he founded during his episcopate. He died in 862 and was buried, at his request, in a cemetery near the Minster, but his relics were moved into the cathedral at Winchester just over a century later, on 15 July 971.

Many miraculous cures were recorded on that day and there was an unusually heavy fall of rain. For this reason Swithun is invoked against drought, and a tradition grew up that wet weather on 15 July would persist for a further 40 days.

✛

852 bishop of Winchester; 862 died
FEAST DAY: 2 July
CULT: Began in 971 when relics were translated
to Winchester cathedral;
popular in England and to a lesser extent
in Scandinavia in Middle Ages

✛

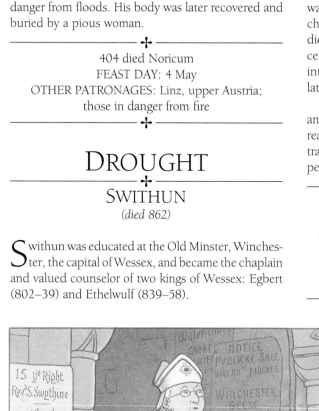

✛

This humorous portrayal of Swithun is based on the belief that if it rains on 15 July—the date on which his relics were translated to Winchester cathedral—wet weather will continue for the next 40 days. The historical Swithun was an influential member of the Wessex court and famous for his charitableness. His shrine was destroyed during the Reformation and restored in 1962.

✛

FAMINE
✛
WALBURGA
(c. 710–779)

Walburga was an Anglo-Saxon missionary who became part of German folklore when the celebration of one of her feast days, 1 May, merged with traditions of pagan revelries at the start of summer to create Walpurgisnacht—the night of a witches' sabbath. Trained as a nun at the double monastery—for monks and nuns—of Wimborne in Dorset, she, with her two brothers Winnibald and Willibald, were leading figures in St. Boniface's mission to convert Germany. She went to the Abbey of Bischofsheim where she became skilled in medicine, and later became abbess of the double monastery of Heidenheim founded by Winnibald. When he died in 761 she assumed sole control of the community of monks and nuns, which she ruled until her death in 779.

Walburga's invocation against famine—one of her emblems is three ears of corn—probably derives from the association of her cult with that of the earlier one of mother earth (Walborg).

✛
---

c. 710 born; 761 abbess of Heidenheim; 779 died
Heidenheim
FEAST DAY: 25 February
ALSO KNOWN AS: Walpurgis; Vaubourg
CULT: In Germany, Flanders, France from
the ninth century
EMBLEMS: Three ears of corn; crown, scepter;
phial of oil

✛

PLAGUE
✛
CATALD
(seventh or eighth century)

Catald is said to have been an Irish monk who was born in Munster, Ireland, and was educated at the monastery of Lismore, where he later became a teacher himself.

He went on pilgrimage to the Holy Land. On his return journey he was shipwrecked near Taranto, in southern Italy, where its people eventually chose him as their bishop. He is believed to have remained there until his death some 15 years later.

He is one of southern Italy's most efficacious saints, with a reputation for curing many ills.

He is invoked against plague because the village of Roccoromana has been free from this and other epidemics since the fifteenth century—an immunity attributed to his protection—and because he also interceded to save another village, Corato, from the disease in 1483.

✛

Seventh or eighth century, said to have been a
bishop of Taranto
FEAST DAY: 10 May
ALSO KNOWN AS: Cathal
CULT: Centered on Taranto; southern Italy, Sicily,
Malta; the Crusader states in the Holy Land since
the eleventh century
OTHER PATRONAGE: Taranto
ALSO INVOKED: Against drought; storms;
paralysis; blindness; epilepsy; hernia

✛

PILGRIMAGE SITES

✛

*Journeys to the holy places of Christianity are still a part of
religious life today. These photographs show two long-standing
centers of pilgrimage—Saint Peter's in Rome and St. James of
Compostela—and a comparatively modern one: Lourdes.*

*ABOVE Worshippers by the reliquary in St. James
Cathedral in Santiago di Compostela, Spain. The
cathedral stands over the site of James the Great's tomb,
miraculously revealed in the ninth century.*

*Rome is Europe's principal shrine, sacred to both
St. Peter and St. Paul. Saint Peter's, in its Vatican City
(ABOVE AND RIGHT) is Western Christendom's most
important church and contains Peter's relics. It stands
where, according to tradition, the saint was crucified in
67. Since 1300, popes have decreed special "holy years"
for pilgrimages to Rome, originally every 50 years and
then at 25-year intervals. The most recent was 1975.*

RIGHT "The Virgin of the Grotto" at Lourdes, France. The Virgin Mary is said to have appeared to St. Bernadette 18 times in 1858 and to have revealed to her a spring whose waters have the power of curing ills—the magnet that draws millions of pilgrims to Lourdes each year.

BELOW The basilica at Lourdes, focal point of modern Europe's greatest pilgrim movement. The building was consecrated in 1876, 18 years after St. Bernadette's visions, but the saint was not present at the ceremony; she had joined the convent of the Sisters of Notre-Dame ten years earlier.

SHRINES

⁘

Some shrines are containers for saints' relics; others are their tombs. But every shrine is the focal point for a saint's cult—the place where people come to revere the saint or pray for him or her to intercede with God on their behalf.

LEFT *St. Swithun's shrine in Winchester cathedral, England, was rebuilt in 1962 after being destroyed during the Reformation. The original shrine was popular with pilgrims in the Middle Ages.*

ABOVE *St. David's relics are contained in his shrine in St. David's Cathedral, Wales. The saint was a major figure in Welsh Christianity and, in 1120, Pope Callistus II decreed that two pilgrimages to his shrine were equal to one to Rome.*

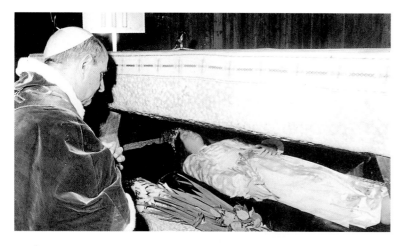

LEFT *The shrine of St. Maria Goretti, Nettuno, near Rome. Between 30 and 40 miracles have been attributed to her since her death, and her canonization in 1950 was attended by the biggest crowd ever known at such an event.*

BELOW *The shrine of St. Vincent de Paul in the Chapelle des Lazaristes, Paris. The saint is revered for the charitableness and devotion to others that characterized his life.*

INDEX OF SAINTS
✛

All the saints featured in this volume are listed here in alphabetical order, for easier and quicker reference. Page numbers refer only to main entries. Names of saints are also included in the main Index of the book.

ABOVE The Blessed Virgin Mary embracing her mother Anne.

RIGHT Catherine of Alexandria and Agnes with her emblem, a lamb.

✧

LEFT Francis of Assisi founded the Franciscan Order in 1210. Clare of Assisi joined him in 1215.

BELOW St. Jerome in a cardinal's robe, with St. Francis.

The apostles Peter, Paul and John with Zeno, bishop of Verona.

INDEX OF PATRONAGES
✢

Alphabetical list of all patronages and invocations—and their saint—mentioned in this book. Names in bold print are those of saints featured under a main entry.

CALENDAR OF FEAST DAYS

✤

Feast Days given here refer only to saints mentioned in this book. The date is usually the date of the saint's death—known as a feast day because death was the beginning of life in heaven—or of the translation of his or her relics, and follows the revised Roman Calendar of 1969. Feast Days are also known as Name Days and, in countries with a strong Catholic tradition, are sometimes celebrated instead of birthdays.

JANUARY
✤

3	Geneviève
13	Kentigern
20	Sebastian
21	Agnes
26	Paula
28	Thomas Aquinas
30	Aldegonda
31	John Bosco

FEBRUARY
✤

2	Blessed Virgin Mary (Purification)
3	Blaise
5	Agatha
8	Jerome Emiliani
9	Apollonia
12	Julian the Hospitaller
14	Valentine
22	Margaret of Cortona
23	Polycarp
25	Walburga

MARCH
✤

1	David
7	Perpetua
8	John of God
9	Frances of Rome
17	Gertrude of Nivelles; Patrick
19	Joseph (see also 1 May)
23	Turibius
25	Blessed Virgin Mary (Annunciation); Dismas

APRIL
✤

2	Francis of Paola
5	Vincent Ferrer
7	John-Baptist de la Salle
12	Zeno of Verona
16	Benedict Joseph Labre; Bernadette (often 18 February in France)
19	Expeditus
21	Beuno
22	Theodore of Sykeon
23	George
25	Mark
27	Zita
29	Catherine of Siena

RIGHT John the Baptist

MAY
✤

1	Joseph (see also 19 March)
4	Florian
7	Notkar Balbulus
10	Antoninus of Florence; Catald
12	Pancras
15	Dymphna
16	Brendan the Navigator; John of Nepomuk; Honoratus
17	Madron
19	Dunstan; Ivo
22	Rita
28	Bernard of Montjoux
30	Ferdinand III of Castile; Hubert of Liège

JUNE
✤

1	Justin
2	Elmo
3	Kevin
8	Médard
9	Columba
13	Antony of Padua
15	Vitus
21	Aloysius Gonzagua
29	Paul; Peter

JULY
✤

2	Blessed Virgin Mary (Visitation); Swithun
3	Thomas
4	Elizabeth of Portugal
6	Maria Goretti
11	Benedict
13	Margaret of Antioch (in the East)
14	Camillus de Lellis

19	Justa and Ruffina		26	Cosmas and Damian		

19 Justa and Ruffina
20 Wilgefortis
22 Mary Magdalene
23 Bridget of Sweden; Phocas
25 Christopher; James the Great
26 Anne
29 Martha
31 Neot

AUGUST

1 Friard
10 Laurence
11 Clare of Assisi
13 Hippolytus
14 Maximilian Kolbe
15 Blessed Virgin Mary
   (Assumption)
16 Roch
19 Sebald
23 Rose of Lima
24 Bartholomew; Ouen
25 Genesius
27 Monica
28 Augustine of Hippo
29 John the Baptist
30 Fiacre
31 Raymond Nonnatus

SEPTEMBER

1 Giles
2 Agricola of Avignon
3 Gregory the Great
7 Gratus of Aosta
8 Blessed Virgin Mary (Nativity)
9 Peter Claver
10 Nicholas of Tolentino
17 Lambert of Maastricht
18 Joseph of Copertino
19 Januarius (see also
   16 December)
21 Matthew
22 Maurice

26 Cosmas and Damian
27 Vincent de Paul
28 Wenceslas
29 Gabriel the Archangel;
   Michael the Archangel
30 Jerome

OCTOBER

1 Theresa of Lisieux
4 Francis of Assisi
6 Faith
10 Gereon
16 Gall
17 Ignatius of Antioch
18 Luke
21 Ursula and her Companions
25 Crispin and Crispinian
28 Jude
31 Wolfgang

LEFT Francis of Assisi

NOVEMBER

2 Eustace (in the East)
5 Kea; Martin de Porres
6 Leonard of Noblac
8 Four Crowned Martyrs
11 Martin of Tours
13 Homobonus; Stanislaus Kostka
15 Albert the Great
17 Gregory the Wonderworker;
   Hugh of Lincoln;
   Martyrs of Paraguay
20 Edmund of East Anglia
22 Cecilia
23 Felicity
25 Catherine of Alexandria
   (suppressed in 1969)
30 Andrew

DECEMBER

1 Eloi
2 Bibiana
4 Barbara; Osmund
6 Nicholas of Myra
7 Ambrose
8 Blessed Virgin Mary
   (Immaculate Conception)
13 Lucy
16 Januarius (see also
   19 September)
26 Stephen
27 John the Apostle

GLOSSARY
✝

Albigensian: belonging to the heretical Albigensian (after the town of Albi in Gascony) or Cathar sect which flourished in southern France in the twelfth and thirteenth centuries.

Annunciation: the Angel Gabriel's announcement to the Blessed Virgin Mary that she would bear Jesus Christ, celebrated on 25 March.

Arianism: heretical doctrine originated by a Libyan theologian, Arius (d. 336) and outlawed in 381.

Ascension: the 40th day after Easter; Christ's ascension into heaven.

Assignation (of patronage): legal assignment.

Assumption: the taking-up into heaven of the Blessed Virgin Mary, celebrated on 15 August.

Beatification: a stage in the process of canonization, involving a declaration by the pope that the candidate is enjoying heavenly bliss and can be venerated locally.

Canon: a cleric attached to a cathedral or church, either living in a community like a monk, or holding estates known as prebends.

Canonization: a solemn definitive act by which the pope admits a candidate into the calendar of saints.

Consecration: the act of dedicating to a sacred purpose.

Cult: veneration (or honoring) of a saint expressed in public acts, local or universal, and formally approved by the pope.

Deacon: minister of the Church ranking below bishop and priest.

Diocese: district under the care and jurisdiction of a bishop.

Doctors of the Church: saints whose writings on doctrine have a special authority; recognized by the pope.

Gnosticism: mystical religion drawing in some elements of Christianity which flourished in the third century.

Martyr: someone who chooses death rather than to renounce the Christian faith.

Nativity: birth (of Jesus, the Blessed Virgin Mary, or John the Baptist).

Novitiate: time of probation and education for those joining a religious order.

Passover: Jewish spring feast commemorating the Exodus from Egypt.

Precentor: important dignitary of a cathedral or monastery.

Preferment: advancement.

Prior: high-ranking officer of a religious house or order.

Priscillianism: heretical movement following the ideas of the Spanish theologian Priscillian (d. 385); popular in Spain from the fourth to the sixth century.

Purification: ceremonial cleansing of a woman after childbirth.

Relics: bodily remains—or belongings—of a saint which become the object of a cult authorized by the pope.

See: seat signifying the office of bishop or pope.

Tertiary: a lay person belonging to a religious order, who lives a holy life in the community rather than observing a strict religious rule; thus member of the Third Order.

Third Order: see Tertiary.

Translation: to move a body—or relics—from one place to another.

Veneration: reverence for a person or object.

Vicar: deputy in a religious office; local parish priest deputizing for a rector or parson.

Vicar-General: a bishop's representative or assistant in matters of law or administration.

Visitation: an ecclesiastical inspection, as when a bishop carries out a visitation of his diocese. The feast of the Visitation (2 July) celebrates the Blessed Virgin Mary's visit to her cousin Elizabeth who hailed her as the mother of the Lord.

BIBLIOGRAPHY
—✛—

Acta Sanctorum. 67 vols, Potthast: Bibliotheca Historica, 1643–(continuing)

Attwater, D. *The Penguin Dictionary of Saints*. New York: Penguin USA, 1984

Attwater, D. *Saints of the East*. New York: P. J. Kennedy and Sons, 1963

Baring-Gould, S. and J. Fisher. *The Lives of the British Saints*. 4 vols. Cambridge: James Clark Co., Ltd, 1907–13

Baudrillart, A., et al., eds. *Dictionnaire d'Histoire et de Géographie Ecclésiastiques*. Paris: Letouzey et Ané, 1912–(continuing)

Bentley, J. *A Calendar of Saints: The Lives of the Principal Saints of the Christian Year*. New York: Facts On File Inc., 1986

Bibliotheca Sanctorum. 12 vols. Rome: Istituto Giovanni, 1961–70

Brewer, E.C. *A Dictionary of Miracles*. Philadelphia: J.B. Lippincott Co., 1934

Brown, P. *The Cult of the Saints, its Rise and Function in Latin Christendom*. Chicago: University of Chicago Press, 1981

Brown, R.E., et al., eds. *The Jerome Biblical Commentary*. Englewood Cliffs, N. J.: Prentice-Hall Inc., 1968

Butler, A. *The Lives of the Fathers, Martyrs and Other Saints*. 4 vols. New York: P.J. Kennedy and Sons, 1895

Cabrol, F., and H. Leclercq, eds. *Dictionnaire d'Archéologie Chrétienne et de Liturgie*. 15 vols. Paris: Letouzey et Ané, 1907

Campenhausen, H. von. *The Fathers of the Greek Church*. Trans. S. Goodman. New York: Pantheon Books, 1959

Campenhausen, H. von. *The Fathers of the Latin Church*. Trans. M. Hoffmann. London: A. & C. Black, 1964

Cross, F.L., and E.A. Livingstone, eds. *Oxford Dictionary of the Christian Church*. 2d ed. New York: Oxford University Press, Inc., 1974

Delaney, J.D. *Dictionary of Saints*. New York: Doubleday, 1982

Delehaye, H. *Les Origines du Culte des Martyrs*. Bruxelles: Bureaux de la Société des Bollandistes, 1912

Delehaye, H. *The Legends of the Saints*: Trans. D. Attwater. New York: Forham University Press, 1962

Doble, G.H. *The Saints of Cornwall*. Chatham: Barrett & Neves, 1960

Farmer, D.H. *The Oxford Dictionary of Saints*. 3d ed. New York: Oxford University Press, Inc., 1993

Gibson, M. *Saints of Patronage and Invocation*. Bristol: Avon County Library, 1982

Head, T. *Hagiography and the Cult of Saints*. New York: Cambridge University Press (American branch), 1990

Holweck, F.G. *Biographical Dictionary of the Saints*. St Louis, Mo.: B. Herder Book Co., 1924

Kelly, J.N.D. *The Oxford Dictionary of Popes*. New York: Oxford University Press, Inc., 1985

Kemp, E.W. *Canonisation and Authority in the Western Church*. London: Oxford University Press, 1948

Lobineau, F.A. *Les Vies des Saints de Bretagne*. 5 vols. Paris: Méquignon, 1836–8

Millard, B., ed. *The Book of Saints ... Compiled by the Benedictine Monks of St. Augustine's Abbey, Ramsgate*. 6th ed. London: A. & C. Black, 1989

New Catholic Encyclopaedia. 15 vols. New York: McGraw-Hill Book Co., 1967

Post, W.E. *Saints, Signs and Symbols*. Wilton, Conn.: Morehouse Publishing Co., 1974

Reed, O. *An Illustrated History of Saints and Symbols*. Bourne End, Bucks: Spurbooks, 1978

Röeder, H. *Saints and their Attributes*. London: Longmans, Green and Co., 1955

Ryan, G., and H. Ripperger, trans. *The Golden Legend of Jacobus de Voragine*. London and New York: Longmans, Green and Co., 1941

Thurston, H., ed. *Butler's Lives of the Saints*. Tunbridge Wells: Burns, Oates & Washbourne Ltd, 1956

Tommasini, A. *Irish Saints in Italy*. Trans. J.F. Scanlan. London, Glasgow: Sands and Co., 1937

Walsh, M., ed. *Butler's Lives of Patron Saints*. New York: Harper & Row Publishers, 1991

Williams, C. *Saints, Their Cults and Origins*. 1980

Woodward, K.L. *Making Saints: Inside the Vatican*. New York: Simon & Schuster, 1990

INDEX

Note: Patronages will be found in the Index of Patronages on pages 171–75
Page numbers in *italics* indicate illustrations

ACKNOWLEDGEMENTS

ILLUSTRATION CREDITS

T = TOP   B = BELOW   C = CENTRE   L = LEFT   R = RIGHT

Agnew & Sons, London/Bridgeman Art Library, London 111B; Ashmolean Museum 90; Barber Institute, Birmingham/Bridgeman Art Library, London 145B; Bonhams, London/Bridgeman Art Library, London 18L, 22; Burghley House/Bridgeman Art Library, London 129; Jean-Loup Charmet 10, 12R, 15, 16, 17, 36, 39, 49, 57, 58R, 62, 67L, 67R, 69, 70L, 70R, 73B, 74, 77, 78, 79, 80, 85, 93, 95, 98B, 106, 107, 114, 115, 124T, 127, 135L, 137, 140, 148R, 152, 154L, 155, 156T, 156B, 159R, 167B, 168R; Christies, London/Bridgeman Art Library, London 83, 96, 144T, 170; Christies Colour Library 116L; Roger Cracknell/Trip 34R, 166L, 166R; Museo. Diocesano, Cortona/Bridgeman Art Library, London 60TR; C. M. Dixon 14L, 20R, 42B, 59T, 86, 98TR, 145, 168L; Paul Elek Ltd 41T; ET Archive 6, 33, 34L, 35, 47, 53, 60TL, 61TL, 61R, 71, 99, 120, 128B, 142L, 143B, 147, 169; Mary Evans Picture Library 11, 12L, 13, 14BR, 21, 23BL, 25, 26, 31, 32, 37, 40, 41B, 44, 46L, 48, 51, 52B, 54, 58L, 63, 65L, 81, 84, 89, 92L, 92R, 94, 97, 98TL, 101, 104R, 108, 109, 110, 111T, 113TL, 113TR, 116R, 130, 131T, 131B, 134, 135R, 136, 142R, 146, 157T, 159L, 160, 162, 165T; Eye Ubiquitous/Trip 23R, 73T, 165B; Fitzwilliam Museum, Cambridge/Bridgeman Art Library, London 169B; Galleria Degli Uffizi/Bridgeman Art Library, London 60B, 72L, 124B; Giraudon/Bridgeman Art Library, London 30, 46R, 61BL, 82L; Hatton Gallery, University of Newcastle Upon Tyne/Bridgeman Art Library, London 176, 177; Hermitage/Bridgeman Art Library, London 122; J. Highet/Trip 82R; Sarah Howerd 117, 132BR; Hulton Deutsch 104L, 167T; The Hutchison Library 14TR, 20L, 27; Kunsthistorisches Museum/Bridgeman Art Library, London 119L; Louvre, Paris/Bridgeman Art Library, London 42T, 68; Magyar Nemzeti Galeria/Bridgeman Art Library, London 18R, 119R;

Derick McGroarty/Trip 154R; Steve Marwood 23TL; Roy Miles Gallery/Bridgeman Art Library, London 65R; National Gallery/Bridgeman Art Library, London 87, 88, 132BL; National Gallery of Scotland/Bridgeman Art Library, London 112; Ognissanti, Florence/Bridgeman Art Library, London 64; Ann & Bury Peerless 143T, 145T; Phillips Auctioneers/Bridgeman Art Library, London 45; Pinacoteca Di Brera, Milan/Bridgeman Art Library, London 133; Prado, Madrid 139; Prado, Madrid/Bridgeman Art Library, London 52T; Private collection/Bridgeman Art Library, London 163; Pushkin Museum/Bridgeman Art Library, London 59BR, 128TL; Richardson & Kailas Icons, London/Bridgeman Art Library, London 56T; Helene Rogers/Trip 91L; Museo Di San Marco Dell'Angelico, Florence/Bridgeman Art Library, London 132T; Scala 126; South American Pictures 28, 29, 103; Trip 72R, 73T, 82R, 148L; Unterlinden Museum, France/Bridgeman Art Library, London 43, 61R, 121; By courtesy of the Board of Trustees of The V & A/Bridgeman Art Library, London 113B, 128TR, 144B; Vatican/Bridgeman Art Library, London 19; Christopher Wood Gallery, London/Bridgeman Art Library, London 125; York City Art Gallery/Bridgeman Art Library, London 161; Zefa 100, 157B, 164L, 164TR, 164BR.

NOTE: The publishers have made every effort to trace copyright holders for illustrations which appear in this book and wish to offer their apologies for any unintentional errors or omissions.

EDDISON · SADD
Editors   Elizabeth Hallam, Tessa Clark and Cecilia Walters
Proof Reader   Nikky Twyman
Indexer   Dorothy Frame
Designer   Sarah Howerd
Picture Researcher   Liz Eddison
Production   Hazel Kirkman and Charles James